The Plan
(and Other Plans)

By Bridie Connell and Grace Rouvray

CURRENCY PRESS
The performing arts publisher

HotHouse
THEATRE

CURRENT THEATRE SERIES

First published in 2024
by Currency Press Pty Ltd,
Gadigal Land, Suite 310, 46–56 Kippax Street, Surry Hills, NSW 2010, Australia
enquiries@currency.com.au
www.currency.com.au

in association with HotHouse Theatre

Typeset by Brighton Gray for Currency Press.
Cover image by Michelle Higgs
Front cover shows Bridie Connell and Grace Rouvray.

Currency Press acknowledges the Traditional Owners of the Country on which we live and work. We pay our respects to all Aboriginal and Torres Strait Islander Elders, past and present.

NATIONAL LIBRARY OF AUSTRALIA

A catalogue record for this book is available from the National Library of Australia

Contents

The Plan (and Other Plans) was developed and produced by HotHouse Theatre, premiering at The Butter Factory Theatre, Wodonga on 19 March 2024 with the following company:

GEN	Grace Rouvray
ROSIE	Bridie Connell
DAD (HAMISH)	PJ Williams
MUM (CAROLYN)	Kerryn Beatty
TONY	Damian Callinan
ARLO / MARKUS	Nick Steain

Director, Karla Conway
Production Designer, Sophie Woodward
Composer & Sound Designer, Andree Cozens
Lighting Designer, Jasper Wood
Dramaturgy, Karla Conway
Stage Manager, Maisy Butchart
Producer, Beck Palmer

CHARACTERS

GEN, female, early 30s.

ROSIE, female, late 20s.

DAD (HAMISH), male, mid–late 50s.

CAROLYN, female, mid–late 50s.

TONY, male, 50s/60s.

SUGGESTED DOUBLING

TONY—DR. NILSEN, BINGO ANNOUNCER, ANNOUNCER 3, ANNOUNCER 5, JAZZ SINGER, TREVOR GOODWINKLE, HIGH-SCHOOLER 2, HIGH-SCHOOLER 4, SCOTT RILEY.

CAROLYN—KYLIE, DEB, ANNOUNCER 1, ANNOUNCER 2, ANNOUNCER 4, JAZZ SINGER, MADAME BURGESS, HIGH-SCHOOLER 1, HIGH-SCHOOLER 3, HIGH-SCHOOLER 5.

NOTES

The actors playing Carolyn and Tony also play an assortment of other roles. The actors playing Gen, Rosie and Hamish only appear as their roles. Markus and Arlo are voices only, it is preferable these are voiced by a male 28–35.

This is a world with ambitious staging. Directors are encouraged to be as ingenious as they like to achieve it. The world can be stripped back or followed down to the last prop.

The type of cancer Hamish suffers is intentionally never specified. Actors playing Hamish can detail their own approach.

The songs sprinkled throughout are intended to evoke nostalgia, warmth and are reminiscent of listening as a child from the backseat on a long car trip. We have used Paul Kelly as an artist who encapsulates these feelings for us, but encourage future directors to change the artist and songs to find that feeling for themselves.

This play text went to press before the end of rehearsals and may differ from the play as performed.

SCENE ONE

Hamish's house. A living room in a regional town. A record player in a corner. There's a Paul Kelly record on a shelf next to a stack of gardening books. Two women enter. They are ROSIE *and* GEN, *and they look extremely serious. In an overly dramatic tone:*

ROSIE: Ready to go in?
GEN: No.
ROSIE: I'll go with you.
GEN: I can't.
ROSIE: Why?

> GEN *turns to the audience and speaks with a cinematic level of drama.*

GEN: Because someone is going to die.
ROSIE / GEN: [*echoing in a whisper*] Die … die … die …

> ROSIE *clicks her fingers and suddenly everything is more Christmassy and upbeat.*

ROSIE: Okay, so it's Christmas—
GEN: Rosie, no-one knows who we are.
ROSIE: I'm Rosie.
GEN: I'm Gen, and we are—
ROSIE / GEN: Sisters.
ROSIE: So it's Christmas, which means it's me, Gen, Dad, Mum and our stepdad Tony.
GEN: Mum and Dad have now been divorced longer than they were together.
ROSIE: About five years ago we started to have Christmas all together at Dad's house.
GEN: It's deeply uncomfortable.
ROSIE: It's a blended family—
GEN: It's weird!
ROSIE: Mum likes us all together—
GEN: Does she? Is that why she moved to France when we were kids?
ROSIE: Gen! [*To audience*] It was a secondment, for ten months.

GEN: Mum became obsessed with *Modern Family* and has since forced us into a perfect, happy, blended family, and the best place to be a perfect, happy, blended family is Dad's. Because he has a pool.

> *Beat.*

So it's Christmas Day.

ROSIE: Our typical Christmas is—

GEN: Chaos—

ROSIE: Lively—

GEN: Family screaming—

ROSIE: The whole family together—

GEN: Passive-aggression—

ROSIE: Unnecessary comments—

> *They cheesily signal to the audience like an HSC drama presentation.*

ROSIE / GEN: And … TENSION!

ROSIE: Mum—

GEN: Carolyn, with a 'y'—

ROSIE: —spends the day talking to anyone who will listen about her latest European jaunt, and the various methods of preparing potatoes.

CAROLYN: Jamie says to parboil first for the perfect crunch.

ROSIE: [*to audience*] Jamie is Jamie Oliver, her one true love.

GEN: And although she hasn't lived here in seventeen years she still behaves like this is her house.

CAROLYN: Girls, get the reindeer candles.

> CAROLYN *fusses about getting the table setting just right.*

GEN: Rosie, get the reindeer candles.

ROSIE: [*to audience*] Then there's Dad—

GEN: —local legend, landscape gardener for most of the town, and basically a labrador.

ROSIE: He's just so happy to be there!

GEN: Dad.

> *Beat. No-one appears.*

ROSIE / GEN: [*screaming like they did as kids*] DAAAAAADDDDDDD!

> DAD (HAMISH) *enters and gives the girls an affectionate pat and scruff of their hair.*

DAD: Hi possums!

ROSIE: If you were playing Hamish McMahon bingo, you could guarantee this is being called:

DAD: What's this bloody racket?

> *He tunefully wails the second line of the third verse of 'How to Make Gravy' by Paul Kelly.*

ROSIE / GEN: Death, taxes, Paul Kelly.

> CAROLYN *enters.*

DAD: Merry Christmas, Carolyn.

GEN: [*to audience*] That's Carolyn with a 'y.'

> GEN*'s phone alarm goes off.*

CAROLYN: Hamish, Tony's got the prawns. Deveined.

GEN: Mum, the veggies need to come out of the oven now. [*To audience*] And there's Tony, Mum's new husband.

ROSIE: They've been married for twelve years.

GEN: Mum's new husband. Used to be a pilot. Which I think is what turned Mum on—

ROSIE: [*blocking her ears*] Lalalalala!

GEN: She liked the whole captain thing. They met in a Qantas club in Shanghai.

> TONY *walks in carrying a box of Favourites and some Christmas gifts.* ROSIE *rushes to* TONY *and they have a big hug.* GEN *gives him a perfunctory wave.*

Ooft, get ready for this. [*In a sports-commentator voice*] Ding, ding, ding! And it's Dad versus Stepdad, here comes the most awkward interaction ever between two men who were destined to love the same woman. A story of ego and male pride, get ready for the death blow!

TONY: Hi mate. Merry Christmas!

> *It is a perfectly pleasant interaction and* GEN *looks thrown.* CAROLYN *continues to flutter around the dining-room table.*

DAD: Tony! How are you going?

CAROLYN: Unemployed and under my feet.

TONY: Retired isn't unemployed, love.

DAD: Before you ask!

DAD *holds up a miniature aeroplane.*

TONY: You made it!

DAD: Real fiddly work isn't it.

TONY: Isn't it!

CAROLYN: It's bloody clutter.

They stare at it in awe.

DAD / TONY: The Wright Flyer!

TONY: First ever plane!

DAD: A beauty!

TONY: I bought you this. It's the Qantas B-seven-four-seven-four-hundred. I love surprises

DAD: The old livery?

TONY: Bingo.

ROSIE: When did you get into planes?

DAD: Oh you know, just a casual aviation enthusiast.

DAD *and* TONY *laugh at a seeming in-joke as they exit.*

GEN: TENSION!

ROSIE: There's no tension.

GEN: So it's Christmas Day—

CAROLYN: Rosie, I need to talk to you and Markus about floral arrangements.

ROSIE: Hard pass. So, it's Christ—

GEN: Ahhh Markus.

ROSIE: Don't.

GEN: Markus is Rosie's … I don't even know how to describe him.

ROSIE: Fiancé. That's how you describe him. He's my fiancé.

GEN: Sure. He's just the epitome of nothing to write home about. See. [*Gesturing to nothing*] It's like he's not even here.

ROSIE: [*ignoring* GEN] We've been together for five years and we have a son. Well, his son. My stepson.

GEN: Bluebird.

ROSIE: Fenix.

GEN: I can't call him that.

ROSIE: You have to call him Fenix. It's his name.

GEN: Rosie.

ROSIE: He's a three-year-old.

GEN: It's a stupid name.

ROSIE: He doesn't know he has a stupid name.

GEN: The minute he goes to school he will.

ROSIE: [*to audience*] Markus had a one-night stand BEFORE we started dating, then we got together—

GEN: Sorry, I have to take this. [*On the phone*] Hi. Yes, same to you. Merry merry. Where are we at with Henry?

> ROSIE *sighs, and pushes on. As* GEN *talks on the phone, she rearranges the table place settings and swats away anyone who tries to help.*

ROSIE: [*to audience*] And then after we'd been together for a year or two we found out that there was a—there was Fenix. From the one-night stand. It was … a lovely surprise … for all of us.

CAROLYN: Why doesn't Fenix call you Mum?

GEN: [*on the phone*] That's simply not good enough, Brad.

ROSIE: Because Shelley is his mum.

CAROLYN: Oh.

> *Beat.*

That's okay, you'll have your own soon.

ROSIE: Let the ink dry on my Master's first.

CAROLYN: And the wedding! I have a dress! I'll show you a picture. Also let's talk dates, we can get Sheridan On the Lake, but it'd have to be earlier than you were thinking.

GEN: [*to audience*] Ahh yes, apart from potatoes Mum's other favourite sport is bullying her children into procreation and wedlock. [*On phone*] You too, merry Christmas—

> *She hangs up.*

—and a fucky new fuck, you fuckwit.

CAROLYN: Charming. Are you seeing anyone, Gen?

GEN: Yes.

CAROLYN: REALLY?!

GEN: Yep. Been in a long-term relationship with my job for about five years. Silver anniversary. Bought myself this necklace.

CAROLYN: Don't be like that.

ROSIE: But she's not, not dating. Like you're on the scene. Yeah? Gen?

GEN: Nope.

ROSIE: [*to audience*] I'm really not sure why Gen won't tell me about the guy from her work that I KNOW she is dating.

GEN: We're not dating.

ROSIE: Hooking up?

GEN: That's not what's happening.

ROSIE: Sounds like you need to have the conversation …

GEN: Sounds like you need to shut up.

ROSIE: [*back in HSC drama mode*] Sex! Dating! Peer pressure!

GEN: [*matching the energy*] Fuck off!

ROSIE: So Gen is defensive—

GEN: —I am not defensive!

ROSIE: Gen works in some job that none of us understand but I think her official title is 'Woman Who Spends Time On Phone'.

GEN: Okay—

ROSIE: Hello—Genevieve here. Yes. Work, yes work work. Yes, I am highly important! Mmmmm yes! Great point, let's action that immediately. I simply love meetings. [*Imitating dial tone*] Sorry I got another important call. Hello—yes. Work, yes work work. Oooooh yes, SYNERGY! Buy! Sell!

> *She peters out, feeling* GEN *stare at her.*

GEN: What do you think my job is?

> CAROLYN *re-enters carrying a tray.*

Mum, those are for dessert! They have to go back in the fridge.

> *Gen's phone starts ringing again.* DAD *intermittently sings lyrics from 'How to Make Gravy'.*

CAROLYN: Oh come on, Gen, it's Christmas Day, get off your phone.

GEN: Sorry, but they pay me a lot of money.

ROSIE: Gen is rudely referencing that I am a teacher and am therefore paid as a teacher.

> GEN *answers the phone, barking orders to someone as* CAROLYN *dovetails between the two girls setting the table.*

So it's Christmas Day and apart from … liveliness it's all quite normal.

GEN: Dad switches the carols to PK. We play games—

DAD: Two syllables! Second syllable.

CAROLYN: Sounds like 'hat'. Cat. Rat!

GEN: Tony talks about his new shade awning.

TONY: At two o'clock, hottest part of the day—full sun coverage.

ROSIE: Dad tells us how Mum wouldn't let him name us Pauline and Kelly.

> ROSIE *and* GEN *mouth the words 'No-one would know who Paul Kelly was in thirty years' time', and 'So wrong'.*

DAD: And she thought no-one would know who Paul Kelly was in thirty years' time. She was so wrong.

TONY: [*reading a Christmas-cracker joke*] How did the ornament get addicted to Christmas?

GEN: Mum orders people to do jobs that she'll eventually do herself.

CAROLYN: Tony, the bread rolls go on the left-hand side.

GEN: Rosie, move the salads down this end of the table.

TONY: He was hooked on trees his whole life.

GEN: A lot of lawn chat.

ROSIE: Lots of shrub chat.

CAROLYN: It's not looking lush at all this summer.

DAD: You have to aerate the lawn. I've told you this—

ROSIE: The adults discuss the latest deaths, illness and traumatic life events of various people in the town.

CAROLYN: Did you hear about Poppy Green? Dead.

TONY: That reminds me, Richard Bainbridge? Dead.

GEN: Mum makes us sign the guestbook even though we're her literal children. [*To* CAROLYN] You. Don't. Live. Here!

CAROLYN: Darling, you divorce the man, not the pool.

ROSIE: It's a pretty stock standard Christmas.

GEN: But in about twenty seconds Dad is going to collapse.

ROSIE: You make it sound so dramatic!

GEN: It was dramatic. In twenty-three seconds' time Mum is going to start screaming—

ROSIE: This really was the start of it all.

GEN: Okay and I'm dramatic?

ROSIE: There is drama and truth, Gen, I am truth and you are drama.

GEN: I know you are but what am I—

> *As the girls continue to bicker,* DAD *suddenly collapses and, like clockwork,* CAROLYN *starts to scream. The girls step back into the scene and run toward their dad.*

SCENE TWO

DAD *sits in a hospital bed, flanked by his daughters.* GEN, *still wearing a paper Christmas crown, is buried in her phone googling symptoms.*

GEN: [*reading*] Web MD says 'an unexplained collapse could be a result of a heart attack, stroke, seizure, drug overdose or alcohol poisoning'.

ROSIE: [*fluffing his pillows*] Here, Dad. Sit up.

GEN: How much did you have to drink?

DAD: I didn't drink—

ROSIE: Sit back. How many fingers am I holding up?

DAD: Three.

GEN: Did you have the punch? There was vodka in the punch.

ROSIE: When is Gravy Day?

DAD: [*to* ROSIE] The twenty-first of December. [*To* GEN] It's not alcohol poisoning, sweetheart.

GEN: Do you smell toast? Did you smell toast at any point?

DAD: I did smell toast actually!

ROSIE / GEN: Shit. / When?

DAD: At breakfast. When I made toast. Girls—I'm fine.

> DR NILSEN *enters studying* DAD'*s chart.*

DR NILSEN: Hamish, how are you feeling?

DAD: Feeling much better and ready to go home.

GEN: Doctor Nilsen, we think he has alcohol poisoning.

DAD: Terri, we don't—

ROSIE: [*rummaging through her bag*] Do you want a Berocca? When I'm hungover I have two.

DR NILSEN: Are you up to date with your meds, Hamish?

DAD: Yes.

> *Beat.*

GEN: What meds?

DR NILSEN: What time did you take them?

DAD: Look, I ran out two days ago and thought it would be alright to wait till after Christmas to come in and see you for more.

DR NILSEN: Hamish, you really need to—

ROSIE: What meds?

DR NILSEN: Was it the methotrexate?

DAD: Terri, maybe we—

GEN: [*to audience*] I'm immediately googling methotrexate.

> GEN *is buried in her phone.*

ROSIE: What is methotrexate? Can you spell that please? Dad won't remember the name.

DAD: Let's not—

DR NILSEN: Methotrexate is effective if you take it exactly as prescribed. And you're over the initial side effects now, Hamish. I really need you to commit to it.

GEN: 'Methotrexate is a chemotherapy agent and immune-system suppressant. It is used to treat cancer and ectopic pregnancy.'

> *This sinks in. She looks at* DAD.

Dad, are you pregnant or do you have cancer?

DR NILSEN: [*going to leave*] I'll give you a minute.

GEN: No-one moves.

ROSIE: You have cancer?

> DAD *looks sadly at his girls.*

DAD: Yes.

ROSIE: How long have you known?

DAD: Just for a couple of months.

ROSIE: And you didn't tell us?

DR NILSEN: To be fair, I did suggest he tell you.

ROSIE: Why didn't you tell us?

DR NILSEN: Patient–doctor confidentiality.

ROSIE: Not you, Terri.

DAD: The prognosis is good! I'm going to be fine. Early stages. Plus, you just got engaged to Markus, Gen won her award, no point ruining the mood with something not worth worrying about.

GEN: Not worth worrying about? [*Pretending to make a phone call*] Hey, Cancer Council, turns out we don't need to worry about cancer any more!

ROSIE: Call off the fundraisers!

DAD: I'm going to be fine. It's a shock. I shouldn't have kept it. I'm sorry. But I'm going to be okay.

A long pause, while the girls try to compute. All of a sudden—

ROSIE / GEN: Have you told Mum?

Before DAD can answer—

ROSIE: Does she know?

GEN: She can't know!

ROSIE: Gen, she has to know! We just have to have a strategy for how we tell her—

GEN: The strategy is silence!

ROSIE: We have to tell her!

GEN: Dad, she'd be awful!

ROSIE: Maybe tell her when you've already recovered.

GEN: But then there's no point, just don't tell her.

DAD: Why?

GEN: Because.

ROSIE: [*to audience*] Look, Mum is great.

GEN: Hmmm …

ROSIE: She's just …

GEN: Exactly.

ROSIE: There have been times where she'd—

GEN: She literally uses the drinking game 'Never Have I Ever' to get goss. 'Never have I ever gone wedding-ring shopping.' 'Never have I ever been currently dating someone.' Doesn't even make sense.

Back to DAD—

DAD: Now Gen—

ROSIE: I can't lie! When I lie my eye twitches!

GEN: It's not a lie, it's an omission! Dad, when you tell her, you're telling the whole town. Everyone will know every single test you have ever had and what things have been shoved in what holes. Do you remember when I was fifteen and I had a rash on my …

She motions to her crotch.

DAD: Ah. Yes.

GEN: Well you shouldn't. You shouldn't know about that. I told Mum in confidence.

DR NILSEN: I actually heard about that too.

GEN: Terri heard!

DR NILSEN: And I did not treat that case.

GEN: And he did not treat that case. I'm just saying, this is a family thing. It's the three of us.

DR NILSEN: And me.

GEN: And Terri. Mum doesn't need to be involved.

DAD: Point taken. But she's here in town and company is always nice.

ROSIE: You're not going to be alone, I'll come visit.

DAD: Girls, you're busy—

GEN: I—I could take leave. [*Off* ROSIE's *look*] I could! I'm not too busy for support.

DAD: Maybe—

GEN: Great. Sorted. [*To* DR NILSEN] I will need a schedule of Dad's upcoming procedures and treatments. And names of medications.

DR NILSEN: I would be happy to talk you through the treatment plan.

GEN: I will also need to see your qualifications.

> DR NILSEN *sighs.*

[*Sternly to the three of them*] And no telling Mum.

> *They mumble in reluctant agreement.* CAROLYN *enters holding a 'Get Well Soon' balloon.*

CAROLYN: Hi, darlings. Hamish, how're you feeling?

DAD: I have alcohol poisoning.

SCENE THREE

The hospital morphs into a flurry of movement similar to family Christmas.

ROSIE: [*to audience*] The next few days pass in a flurry of tests, Google searches and a really anti-climactic New Year's Eve.

> DAD *goes to stand up and* CAROLYN *pushes him back into a chair.*

GEN: [*to audience*] Like clockwork, Mum has already inserted herself.

CAROLYN: Hamish, have you heard from Terri today?

The girls run over to their mother.

GEN: [*to audience*] So we run interference.

[*To* CAROLYN] MUM! … Rosie would love to talk to you about her wedding.

CAROLYN *lets a little squeal of excitement out and* ROSIE *looks annoyed at* GEN.

ROSIE: … Yes, I would.

CAROLYN: I'll get my planner!

CAROLYN *runs off.*

ROSIE: [*to audience*] Dad starts another round of treatment—

GEN: He's doing really well, so Rosie and I head home.

ROSIE, *in her kitchen, makes a cup of tea.* GEN *is in her office typing away at her laptop with her airpods in. Beat.*

Now what?

ROSIE: [*to audience*] Gen has many talents, but dealing with real emotions is not one of them, so she decides to deal with our dad having cancer in the only way she knows how: a spreadsheet. She. Loves. A. Plan.

GEN: Have you opened it?

ROSIE: [*sitting down at her laptop*] It's just loading, hang on. Oh yep, got it.

GEN: Great. So, I reckon—

ROSIE: Gen!

GEN: What?

ROSIE: You've called it 'the Cancer Calendar'!

GEN: It is a calendar based around visiting Dad while he recovers from cancer, what am I supposed to call it?

ROSIE: 'The Support Calendar' or something.

GEN: Lame.

ROSIE: I think it's inappropriate.

GEN: I think it's catchy and to the point.

ROSIE: 'Dad-and-Daughter Date Calendar.'

GEN: No, sounds incestuous. Big-sister ruling, it's 'the Cancer Calendar'. There are a lot of dates to fly back for so let me know if you need me to book anything.

ROSIE: Why?

GEN: Well, because you're studying—

ROSIE: I've finished studying.

GEN: Yes, but barely. I'm not trying to be condescending, I'm outraged that teachers aren't paid more—

ROSIE: Gen, I said it's fine—

GEN: —Jeez, calm down.

ROSIE: —You calm—

GEN: —So we're in agreement we don't tell Mum?

ROSIE: [*to audience*] I've been thinking about that—
      [*To* GEN] I've been thinking about that—

GEN: No, Rosie, don't do that.

ROSIE: I know she's hard work—

GEN: Rosie—

ROSIE: But this is big, like—it's cancer.

GEN: I'm aware of that, Rosie.

ROSIE: I know you're angry. I am—

GEN: I'm not angry. This isn't about me or anything. This is about Dad and what's best for his healing process. Isn't that what's most important here?

ROSIE: [*to audience*] Did you see that? 'This isn't about me. This is about Dad.' Genevieve McMahon, military-grade manipulator.

GEN: Excuse you!

ROSIE: [*to audience*] It's not about Dad. It's about Mum. When we were young she got a big-deal secondment in France. We were gonna go once our school year finished but then we had to stay for Dad's work, and then their marriage broke down, and then everything was all super-shit for a while. And Gen has never gotten over it.

GEN: I'm so glad you have gotten over your mother deserting you.

ROSIE: [*to audience*] If you haven't realised, I am the sister who goes to therapy. [*To* GEN] Yes she can be annoying, but she's not stupid. She's going to get suspicious if we suddenly start coming home all the time. What's your answer for that, Genevieve?

GEN: All taken care of, Rosemary. I have a structured, watertight plan for each month to ensure a question-free, guilt-free, Carolyn's-emotions-free experience.

GEN *waits for* ROSIE *to look impressed.* ROSIE *stays silent.*

Six more cycles of treatment, so we need six reasons to visit. We alternate each visit each month with a one-month double-up to throw them off the pattern. Simple.

ROSIE: Right.

GEN: I've got Dad's birthday and Easter. When's your ten-year reunion?

ROSIE: Not until September.

GEN: Damn it. What else? There is literally no other reason to go back.

ROSIE: Mum's birthday.

GEN: Yes … which is Julyyyyyy thirteenthhhhh.

ROSIE: Twenty-third.

GEN: Perfect! That'll be the double. Any wine festivals or something?

ROSIE: What about the Agricultural and Pastoral Show!!

GEN: No. Absolutely not.

ROSIE: It's mid-June. You used to love the A and P show!

GEN: When I was twelve! I can't do June, I'm delivering a campaign.

ROSIE: Oh, I'm so sorry. I'll just tell Dad's cancer cells to take a break mid-June.

GEN: Oh, yeah, also on the twenty-fourth, can you put in 'Go Fuck Yourself'?

ROSIE: There are heaps of things we can come back for, sending now.

GEN *opens the link on her phone.*

GEN: The Lavender, Chilli and Herb Show?

ROSIE: It's in May!

GEN: Rosie, I would rather have cancer than go to that.

ROSIE: What about visiting friends?

GEN: I don't talk to anyone from home any more.

ROSIE: Oooh! I know! Who's having a baby? There's bound to be a couple.

GEN: Yes!

ROSIE: Hang on, I'm on Facebook …

ROSIE *scrolls through her phone.*

Yep! Andrea Chu just posted a sonogram. Perfect. You can go down
    for that.

GEN: Perfect. Wait, what? Why am I going? You can go.

ROSIE: She's from your year.

GEN: You're her Facebook friend!

ROSIE: So are you!

GEN: What? I have literally no memory of this woman. Oh come on,
    she's already had one!

ROSIE: Gen!

GEN: Ugh, I'll do baby shower, you do Lavender, Herb and Chilli.
    Deal?

ROSIE: Deal.

> GEN's boss DEB knocks on the door.

GEN: I've got to go—

ROSIE: Ooh, your work boyfriend there for a meeting?

GEN: What? No. My boss is here. I'll call you back.

ROSIE: You won't call me back!!

GEN: But I'll think about doing it and that's kind of the same thing.
    Byeeee.

ROSIE: Byeee.

> ROSIE keeps drinking tea and texting.

DEB: You wanted to talk?

GEN: Yes … Look, Deb—

DEB: No. You can't—

GEN: What?

DEB: You can't resign. I will literally double whatever they're paying
    you.

GEN: Really?

DEB: Absolutely.

> GEN leans back in her chair to play the game then snaps herself
> out of it.

GEN: No. no. I'm not resigning.

DEB: Oh thank fuck. Don't scare me. What is it then? I've got a Zoom.

GEN: Look … ah … I am just going to say this. My dad is sick. Cancer.

DEB: Shit. Sorry, Gen. How long do you want off?

GEN: I don't want any time off. I just need to work remotely while he's getting treatment.

DEB: We can do that. But you can also have time off, Gen.

GEN: I would prefer to work.

DEB: Gen—

GEN: Can this just stay between us for the moment? I don't want people to look at me with sad faces.

DEB *looks at her with a sad face.*

DEB: Okay. We'll say you're covering someone in the Melbourne office. I love lying. It'll be fun!

GEN: Thanks.

DEB: I'll work on a cover story. Something saucy.

GEN: [*smiling weakly*] Maybe something that incriminates Brad, he's a cock.

DEB: Take care of yourself.

DEB *leaves. A moment alone is too much and* GEN *calls* ROSIE *back.*

ROSIE: Wow. Impressive.

GEN: I know, sister of the year.

Rosie's phone buzzes and she pulls it away to read the text.

ROSIE: Ah this is Markus, I am actually going to have to go. It's date night.

GEN: Which outback steakhouse will it be tonight?

ROSIE *reads the text and sighs.*

ROSIE: Oh. He has to pick up Fenix instead.

Gen's phone buzzes.

GEN: I have to go.

ROSIE: You are actually the worst.

SCENE FOUR

It's a few weeks later. The Cancer Calendar is in full swing.

GEN: [*to audience*] The calendar is locked, and I must say—it is excellent. I am laying the groundwork with gossip about an illicit affair in the Melbourne office.

GEN *picks up her phone and talks to a colleague on the other end.*

I heard she's a yoga teacher … yep … thirty years older than him … yep … yep, on the boardroom table! [*To audience*] What?

> ROSIE *enters carrying a large grocery bag full of green vegetables.*

[*To audience*] Rosie has her first trip back and by this point she's basically an oncologist.

ROSIE: [*to audience*] Nutritionists recommend that cancer patients stick to—

ROSIE / GEN: —a balanced diet of lean proteins, fruits, vegetables, whole grains and low-fat dairy.

> DAD *enters with his own bag of groceries. A brightly coloured cereal box pokes out.*

DAD: [*waving back to someone*] See ya, James! Let me know what Becky says about the gazebo.

GEN: [*to* ROSIE] Hey, cancer police!

ROSIE: [*to* GEN] Yes? [*Annoyed she turned around*] What?

GEN: [*to* ROSIE] What's Dad got?

> *She gasps and takes the cereal out of his bag.*

DAD: Sweetheart—

ROSIE: Phytochemicals. That's what we want.

DAD: Phyto-what? Are you working for NASA now?

ROSIE: Phytochemicals. [*To audience*] He knows what phytochemicals are. He studied plant science at uni. [*To* DAD] Cancer-fighting foods. Berries. Walnuts. Grapes.

DAD: Rabbit food.

ROSIE: I knew you'd say that. I read it in a book, Dad. *Eat Real to Heal.*

DAD: You two are as bad as each other. Gen left me a voicemail last week to check that I had the right kind of celery. 'The right kind of celery', what an oxymoron. I want a steak.

ROSIE: You want plants.

DAD: Marijuana is a plant.

ROSIE: You did not just say that.

DAD: You know I grew up in the seventies, right? Medical marijuana is a thing, Rosie, keep that in mind.

ROSIE: What is happening right now?

> *Local busybody* KYLIE *appears. She's mid-power-walk and carries Shake Weights.*

KYLIE: Rosie!?

ROSIE / GEN: [*to audience*] Ahhh fuck!

ROSIE: Oh, Kylie! Hi! How are you?

GEN: [*to audience*] Kylie, Mum's favourite town gossip, also worked in the office at our high school.

KYLIE: What are you doing back home?

ROSIE / GEN: [*to audience*] We hate her.

ROSIE: Oh, I'm in town for the Motocross Club's annual rally.

KYLIE: [*surprised*] Are you a revhead?

ROSIE: Massively. Vroom vroom.

DAD: [*suppressing a smirk*] She can't get enough of it! What are you riding these days again, love?

> ROSIE *shoots him a look.*

KYLIE: Wow! Hamish McMahon, you're looking very trim.

DAD: Thanks, Kylie.

KYLIE: What are you doing? Intermittent fasting? Sixteen–Eight?

DAD: No.

KYLIE: Fourteen–Ten? Five–Two?

DAD: Just good food and exercise.

KYLIE: I've been meaning to get in touch, my hedges are in need of a good trim. What is your week looking like?

DAD: I am sure I can fit you in.

KYLIE: I bet you can. So what are you doing now, Rosie?

ROSIE: [*to audience*] She doesn't need to ask this because she's one of those weird Boomers who knows everything about you from the Facebook. [*To* KYLIE] I'm a teacher.

GEN: [*to audience*] She knows this.

KYLIE: Oh, really!

DAD: She just did her Master of Education!

GEN: [*to audience*] She knows this!

ROSIE: It's not a big deal—

DAD: Topped her class.

ROSIE: I mean, I got one distinction once—

KYLIE: Congratulations!!

ROSIE: Thank you.

> KYLIE *isn't talking about her Master's. She's noticed* ROSIE*'s engagement ring.*

KYLIE: Is this Felix's baby-daddy?

ROSIE: Fenix. And yes.

KYLIE: Amazing.

DAD: They met through Motocross.

ROSIE: What? [*Realising*] Yes.

KYLIE: When's the wedding?

ROSIE: Haven't set a date.

DAD: Fenix is going to be ring-bearer. He'll drive up the aisle on a tiny motorbike.

KYLIE: Awwwwww. I've seen them on Facebook.

GEN: [*to audience*] There you go.

KYLIE: So cute. Oh it must be so hard with Felix 'cause he's not yours.

ROSIE: [*stronger this time*] It's Fenix.

KYLIE: It'll be different when you have your own. Hang in there. Hamish, I will call you.

DAD: Yep, see you later this week.

KYLIE: Looking forward to it.

ROSIE / DAD: Bye, bye. / See ya.

> KYLIE *power-walks off, hips swinging. Beat.*

ROSIE: Did Kylie Brackburn just … flirt with you?

DAD: Sweetheart, she's only human.

ROSIE: Yuck!

DAD: It's not my fault I'm an Adonis.

ROSIE: Double-yuck!!

SCENE FIVE

ROSIE *addresses the audience and* GEN *and* DAD *sit down in two hospital chairs on the other side of the stage.* GEN *starts a Zoom call. Headphones on, she mutes and unmutes herself as needed.* DAD *is weary and closes his eyes when not talking or looking at* GEN.

ROSIE: [*to audience*] Gen has the next visit and hers is a little more cancery.

GEN: What are they in for?

DAD: [*pointing*] Colon, liver, breast, breast.

GEN: AHHHHH I regret asking. Mostly 'cause it's weird to hear you say 'breast'. Oh shit, that's me. [*Unmuting*] Great idea, Lee. Let's get final sign-off from the ECD.

She mutes herself again.

DAD: You've been on that call for an hour for that one sentence?

GEN: They were presenting to me, Dad. Great thanks, everyone, thanks, Deb. Fuck, I'm muted. Bye! Oh whatever.

GEN *shuts the Zoom meeting and immediately starts texting and smirking.*

ROSIE: Who are you texting?

GEN: No-one.

ROSIE: [*to audience*] I know that face. I saw it for the first time when she claimed to be texting a 'friend' to meet for a 'run' and the next day I went with her to get the 'morning-after pill'. [*To* GEN] Who are you texting, Gen?

GEN: It's work.

ROSIE: Is 'work' hot?

DAD: Busy day, Gen?

GEN: What? Yep … good. Busy.

ROSIE: Don't sext a boy while Dad is having chemo!

GEN: What do you want me to do? Ask him if he can feel the toxic chemicals circulating his body?

ROSIE: No, just be present, be supportive.

GEN: How are you feeling, Dad?

DAD: I'm okay.

GEN *makes a face like 'THERE' to* ROSIE *and she rolls her eyes.*
DR NILSEN *enters.*

DR NILSEN: How are you today, Hamish?

GEN: [*springing into action*] Twenty minutes ago he felt nauseous. It has since subsided but I have also noticed his heart rate fluctuating intermittently.

DR NILSEN *and* DAD *look at each other.*

DR NILSEN: I wouldn't worry about that. If it gets worse you can take—
GEN: Dolasetron.
DR NILSEN: Yes, the nurses told me you asked for that.
GEN: I've done my research.
DR NILSEN: So have I. And resting, yes Hamish? I don't want to see you out on the mower at the Botanic Gardens again.
DAD: But did you see the edges after Brin had a go at them?? Sloppy work. [*Off* DR NILSEN's *look*] Copy that, Terri.

DR NILSEN *leaves.* GEN *is buried in her phone.*

You work too hard, Gen. Very long days. I've been watching.
GEN: Yes, but I love it. And I'm good at it.
DAD: I've no doubt. But there's more to life than work. You have to switch off.
GEN: I don't want to switch off. It's good for my brain. It's how I'm wired.
DAD: You can't draw from the well if you don't fill it. This whole calendar thing—instead of pretending you're here to go to the …

He consults his copy of the calendar.

… CWA Fundraiser, you could actually go.
GEN: What are you doing?
DAD: I'm just suggesting you take up a … wholesome hobby.
GEN: [*suddenly worried*] Is this 'I'm going toward the light' talk?
DAD: No. I just care about you girls.
GEN: I'm fine! Are you fine?
DAD: I'm great. You all worrying, it's the most attention I've ever got.
GEN: Hmmm. Cute.

Gen's phone buzzes and DAD *rolls his eyes.*

[*Pointing at her phone*] Ahh this is wholesome as fuck! Sorry. I'm planning Andrea Chu's baby shower. Admittedly Andrea Chu doesn't know I am planning her baby shower. But she will. And she'll love it.

GEN *types and talks.*

'Hey girllllll! Congrats on baby number two! I'm back for the CWA. LOLLLLLL. We should catch up—'

Gen's phone rings. ROSIE *starts to set up Gen's space on the other side of the stage for Scene Six.*

DAD: Gen.

GEN: I do actually have to take this. Hello, I am only accepting good news. Go on. YES! I knew they would cave. It's going to impact the budget but I can redo it tonight.

> GEN *paces on the phone.* DAD *smiles.*

SCENE SIX

Hamish's house. There are a few coloured sticky dots on various items in the house. GEN *sits cross-legged around her belongings and an open suitcase. A guided meditation plays but an email, an app alert and WhatsApp messages all cut through the calming track.* ROSIE *watches on.*

ROSIE: [*to audience*] I think Gen actually finds it more relaxing to have a soundtrack of work.

> GEN *takes a deep breath again and her phone rings. She opens one eye to look at the screen, declines the call and continues to breathe deeply.*

GEN: [*trying to focus*] I think Gen finds it most relaxing when you shut up.

ROSIE: [*talking in a calming meditation voice*] You have one new email. Subject: work. 'Can we schedule a meeting in order to schedule a meeting? Namaste.'

> *A ding! Whoever rang has left a message.* GEN *snatches up her phone.*

ARLO: [*voicemail*] Hey, Gen.

ROSIE: [*to audience*] THAT'S THE GUY!!

ARLO: [*voicemail*] Haha. So weird I've never heard your voicemail before. You sound so serious. 'I will endeavour to return your call.' I was terrified. This is your personalised Arlo update. [*Singing*] 'Arlo, Arlo, Arlooooooo.' I'm sorry. That was so shit. Um anyway, was just wondering if you're back today? I have left you some voice memos *and* called so I think that makes me a stalker. I was just checking in really. Hadn't heard from you today. The marketing girls said you're online so I know you're not dead. They miss you though! So do I. Not the same around here. And to be honest I'm needing a vent about Brad being a cock again. Ummm you are probably just busy and that's so cool. But maybe something has happened and you need, um, to talk?

> GEN *stops the voicemail and flops onto her childhood single bed. She puts her phone down. Beat. She tries to get back into her meditation.*

ROSIE: [*to audience*] He seems nice. I like him. Gen! Gen! Gen?

> ROSIE *picks up her phone and calls.*

Hey. You okay?

GEN: Yep, yep, I'm good.

ROSIE: How did today—OW!

GEN: What?

ROSIE: I just stepped on a piece of Lego, OW.

GEN: Ah, domestic bliss.

ROSIE: How was today?

GEN: Finding Nemo went well.

ROSIE: [*to audience*] Gen refuses to say the word 'chemo' and is instead referring to Dad's treatment as 'Finding Nemo', the title of an objectively devastating film. [*To* GEN] That's good.

GEN: Dad's being all existential though. Keeps saying nice, caring things.

ROSIE: He always says nice, caring things.

GEN: Nah it's different. It's more, setting me up for a life when he's … you know, whatever. When are you back again?

ROSIE: July twenty-third.

GEN: Oh, what's that?

ROSIE: Mum's birthday!!

GEN: Oh good, that's both of us. I want you to see what I'm seeing. He's not like, sicker. It just feels different. I could be going insane from two weeks of fresh country air. Were you going to drive again? 'Cause I'll pay for your flight.

ROSIE: You don't need to pay for a flight.

GEN: Teacher salary, I'm happy to.

ROSIE: I know you're happy to, thank you, but you don't need to. I'll talk to Markus first though. He's super-quiet every time I talk about leaving. It's really hard with this and Fenix.

GEN: Fucking shut up, Markus.

ROSIE: Yes, I do agree with you on that.

GEN: I am so sexually frustrated.

ROSIE: Wow, okay. Segue.

GEN: It's true.

ROSIE: Hop on country Tinder.

GEN: What, and bang everyone we went to school with ten years ago?

> GEN *puts her phone on speaker and goes through Tinder.*

ROSIE: Yeah. Sounds great.

GEN: Do you and Markus have good sex? I imagine him as someone who makes A LOT of noises?

ROSIE: [*looking over her shoulder*] Gen! You can't ask that!

GEN: Yes I can. What's your sex like?

ROSIE: Not that it's any of your business, it's fine. It's good. You know, it's, yeah, it's good. It's good.

GEN: Wow, it sounds good.

ROSIE: Because it is. Good.

GEN: Oh. My. God!

ROSIE: What? What?

GEN: I just saw Gus on Tinder!!

ROSIE: Gus!! Like Gus Gus??

GEN: The keeper-of-your-virginity Gus.

ROSIE: Wow is he … [*Whispering*] is he hot?

GEN: Oh yeah, he's hot. He—

> *She starts to read his bio.*

—just came back from his backpacking trip through South America. Awww Gus, that's so hot.

ROSIE: Send me a screenshot.

GEN: Already on the way.

ROSIE: I have to go. Good luck with your quest.

GEN: BYEEEEEE.

> ROSIE *receives the screenshot and has a quick look.*

SCENE SEVEN

GEN: [*to audience*] All that talk of Rosie's ex-lover has her rattling in her—

ROSIE: [*to audience*] Gross. We're related.

> ROSIE *takes a breath, undoes a button or two, dims the lights slightly.*

GEN: [*to audience*] Then stop flirting with me.

ROSIE: [*to audience*] Go away, Gen. It's been a lot. Maintaining a relationship when one of us is away either for work or for a sick dad, step-parenting Fenix, getting my Year Twelves across the differences between the subjunctive and indicative. 'Il faut que je boive' not 'Ils boivent'.

> ROSIE *pulls out her phone. We hear it ring and connect to* MARKUS (*whose dialogue can be pre-recorded or voiced offstage*).

MARKUS: Hey, babe. How was work?

ROSIE: Good. You?

MARKUS: Pretty boring conference, to be honest. But nice people.

ROSIE: Well that's good. You look sexy.

MARKUS: What?

ROSIE: I like your shirt.

MARKUS: Nah, I just spilled bolognese over it.

ROSIE: [*persevering*] Then maybe you should take it off.

MARKUS: Nah, it's freezing. The bloody aircon in here—

ROSIE: MAYBE YOU SHOULD TAKE IT OFF, MARKUS.

MARKUS: [*cottoning on*] Oh. Ohhhh! Oh yeah, should I take it off?

ROSIE: I think so.

MARKUS: Rosie, this is hot. This is—you're really turning me on.

ROSIE: Oh yeah?

MARKUS: Yeah. What are you wearing right now?

ROSIE: What? Markus, it's FaceTime. You can see what I'm wearing.

MARKUS: Yeah, but not underneath. Describe it.

ROSIE: [*to audience*] At this point I remember I'm wearing my least sexy bra, date of origin around 2011.

> [*To Markus*] I'm not wearing anything underneath.

MARKUS: Fuck yeah. I think you should take it—

> *The audio glitches.*

—take it—take it—take it—take it—

ROSIE: Markus? Markus, you're cutting out. Can you hear me?

MARKUS: Can you hear me?

ROSIE: Yeah, can you hear me?

MARKUS: Can you hear me?

ROSIE: FUCK. [*To audience*] I just want to have sex, you know?

GEN: [*to audience*] This is actually tragic.

MARKUS: Babe, I'll call you back—you're frozen.

GEN: Cock-blocked by the NBN!

ROSIE: Gen, can you not?

GEN: *Cock-Blocked and Sex-Deprived*, a memoir by Rosie McMahon.

ROSIE: I'll call you—

GEN: She does not remember the touch of a man—

> ROSIE *can't take any more.*

ROSIE: Gen, stop it. [*To audience*] Look, I'll just tell you what happens, shall I? I attempt to seduce my fiancé because intimacy has not exactly been the top priority lately, and it doesn't go well and I end up taking my top off, but then it freezes again in a very unflattering pose and Markus thinks it's hilarious and it really just cuts to the quick of my insecurity about the ever-deepening forehead lines I've developed from all the crying I've been doing worrying over Dad, and then I feel really stupid for even initiating sex and then I have this horrible feeling that I'm putting too much pressure on Markus (who despite what Gen says has many redeeming features) and Fenix, because they're the only secure thing in this shitstorm of a year we're having and I'm really sorry if it's not sexy to choose security over adventure, Gen, but that's where we're at.

> ROSIE *storms off.* GEN *sees she's gone too far. How does she fix this?*
>
> *Pause.*

GEN: [*sheepishly to audience*] I know. She can't not laugh at this. ROSIE!! [*Said in their secret voice*] … love me!

> ROSIE *slowly walks back out.*

ROSIE: No. Not with secret, silly voice.

GEN: [*said in secret silly voice*] I think you look especially pretty when you're so angry.

ROSIE: Gen.

GEN: [*said in secret silly voice*] The prettiest lady in allll the land.

> ROSIE *smiles. She mimics* GEN*'s gremlin-esque position and adopts the voice.*

ROSIE: But I heard you were the prettiest lady in all the land!

GEN: There are two prettiest ladies in all the land.

> *The girls chase each other like mad, laughing gremlins.*

ROSIE: I didn't realise my voice could still do that.

GEN: I'm sorry.

ROSIE: I know. Can you just—

GEN: I know.

> *A little smile. Then the girls give each other a little 'boop' on the nose, the way they've always mended fences after the big fights.*

SCENE EIGHT

GEN, ROSIE *and* DAD *sit down for dinner at the local RSL all-you-can-eat buffet.* DAD *wears a beanie.*

ROSIE: [*to audience*] We're at the RSL two weeks later, or it could be thirty years earlier if the decor is anything to go by.

GEN: We're playing our favourite sport, Wind Up Dad—watch this—

> *Back to the RSL.*

ROSIE: Hey, Gen, what's that great Australian song—you know—

> *She hums 'You're the Voice' by John Farnham.*

GEN: 'Working Class Man'? 'Land Down Under'?

ROSIE / GEN: 'You're the Voice'!

GEN: SUCH a good song. Didn't it win an award?

ROSIE: Well deserved.

DAD: 'You're the Voice' did NOT deserve to win an award, Paul Kelly was absolutely—

ALL: ROBBED at the 1986 Countdown Australia Music Awards.

> *Beat.*

DAD: 'Before Too Long' is a better song.

> *Beat.*

I'm getting jelly.

> DAD *goes to stand up and sits back down.*

Let's try that again.

ROSIE: You okay, Dad?

DAD: Relax, I'm just old.

> GEN *and* ROSIE *watch him walk cautiously.*

ROSIE: He's looking … more frail lately isn't he?

GEN: Well he's sick, Rosie. He's not going to be sprightly.

ROSIE: Gen … [*To audience*] I've been trying to have a few more 'real' chats about Dad's health with Gen, and she responds the only way she knows how—

GEN: [*picking up her phone*] I have to take this. Hello. I sent that two hours ago. I did. Did you check your spam? Ahhh yep, always the way.

> DAD *comes back with jelly for the three of them.* GEN *hangs up.*

DAD: Gen, phone off at the dinner table please.

GEN: Honestly, why would they call me for that?

ROSIE: You love it!

DAD: Now, I have to talk to you girls—

ROSIE: [*immediately panicked*] Why? What? Yes. Sorry. Listening.

DAD: Now I brought you here for two reasons. One, unlimited steak. That's for me. Two, it's a public place and you won't make a scene—

ROSIE / GEN: Why would—

> DAD *puts his finger to his lips to shhhhhh them.*

DAD: I am fine. Nothing is wrong. No interrupting. Deal?

ROSIE / GEN: Deal.

DAD: I have to start a cycle of immunotherapy—

ROSIE / GEN: WHAT! WHAT DOES THAT MEAN? / YOU WERE MEANT TO BE DONE!

> DAD *puts his finger to his lips to shhhhhh them again.*

DAD: Girls. Public place. George, how ya going, mate? Retaining wall is almost finished. Bloody beauty.

He turns back to the girls.

It's all good news. It's just one final thing to really blow the cobwebs out of the corners.

ROSIE: The cancer cobwebs?

GEN: Nah, the cancer corners.

ROSIE: No, Gen. No—the cancer is the cobwebs, and Dad is the … structure … with the corners that need to be … cleaned.

DAD: That's right. Thank you, possum. Now I know you have your whole schedule—

GEN: Cancer Calendar—

DAD: —Cancer Calendar, and you don't want to involve your mother—

GEN: Does she know? Have you told her? Oh my god, Dad!

ROSIE: Maybe it's a good thing? I still think—

GEN: Absolutely not!

ROSIE: You're denying the woman a chance to talk about another ill person.

GEN: She'd hover and come over allllll the time. 'Just popping in, just popping in. Hello!! Just popping in!!'

He shushes them again.

DAD: This is not about your mother! I was thinking … we could add a couple more events to the calendar.

He smiles a big dorky DAD *smile and from a paper bag pulls out three scarves for each of them. One of them is decidedly shabbier than the other two.*

You are now proud supporters of … THE CRIMSON HUSKIES!

From somewhere in the RSL comes a howl of support, DAD *howls back. This seems to happen anytime someone mentions the Huskies in town.*

I've been supporting the Huskies for years and you'd rather go to the Lavender, Chilli and Herb Show? Now that's just being cruel.

ROSIE: Dad, noooo.

GEN: Oh yes.

ROSIE: [*to audience*] Gen's a big fan of the Huskies or more specifically Jacob Rigeon, midfielder circa 2009.

GEN: [*to audience*] We had sex.

ROSIE: [*to audience*] No you didn't.

GEN: [*to audience*] We made out.

ROSIE: [*to audience*] No you didn't.

GEN: [*to audience*] He scored a goal for me.

ROSIE: [*to audience*] He briefly glanced at you after scoring a goal. Or he was squinting at the sun? We could never be sure.

GEN: We're in.

DAD: Just pull the tags off. There you go.

> *Paul Kelly music begins.*

ROSIE: Fine.

DAD: Grand final's coming up.

ROSIE: Wouldn't miss a game.

SCENE NINE

The music swells and a dreamy montage begins as the trio whips through the Cancer Calendar. GEN, ROSIE *and* DAD *rise and put their scarves on. Suddenly the RSL becomes an oval. They shout and cheer from the sidelines.*

GEN: [*to audience*] Dad adds ten more dates to the calendar. Starting with—oh come on!

DAD: High tackle. Give him fifty!

ROSIE: Exactly what they said!

> *The girls cheer.* DAD *looks chuffed.*

[*To audience*] There's a lot of cups of tea.

GEN: [*to audience*] And RSL dinners.

ROSIE: [*to audience*] Then we get a little … creative.

> *Suddenly we're at the country show, highland-dance division. Scottish music momentarily cuts through Paul Kelly.*

> DAD *and* GEN *strike a pose, ready to dance.*

ANNOUNCER 1: That was Shirley and Darren MacNamara with the sword dance. Up next we have Hamish McMahon and his daughter Gen for the Highland Fling.

> ROSIE *poses proudly holding a sponge cake. A* CWA-TYPE *presents her with a first-place ribbon. She beams and* DAD *snaps a photo of her.*

KYLIE *is back, Shake Weights in tow. She leads* GEN, DAD *and* ROSIE *in a power-walk, hips swinging, or maybe it's an aerobics class.*

A cowboy-hat-wearing dance instructor teaches GEN, ROSIE *and* DAD *in a line-dancing class. They attempt to copy a grapevine and scissor step. It is not slick.*

Another announcer with a bingo ball cage walks across the stage.

BINGO CALLER: Two fat ladies!

ROSIE / GEN: How dare you! / Fuck you!

Yet another announcer—

ANNOUNCER 2: Welcome to the Lavender, Chilli and Herb Show!

DAD *produces a bag of marshmallows! The trio sits down to burn them around a campfire.*

ANNOUNCER 3: It's casino beef week!

ROSIE *puts on a Motocross helmet, acting like she's the star of an action movie.*

GEN, ROSIE *and* DAD *try the grapevine and scissor step again. It is slicker.*

DAD *dabs sweat from his brow.*

GEN *holds a microphone and is mid-speech at Andrea Chu's baby shower.*

GEN: [*emotionless*] As soon as I heard Andrea was pregnant … again … I was deeply … moved. What a terrific mother she will be … again.

DAD *and* ROSIE *wave at Fenix over FaceTime.*

ANNOUNCER 4: And the Crimsons Huskies win the grand final!!

Cheers and howls!

ANNOUNCER 5: That brings the total to twenty-five thousand for the Farmers' Association. Well done everyone. Here to collect the cheque is festival coordinator, Gen McMahon.

DAD *claps his hands excitedly, and snaps another photo before moving to sit down in a chair as* DR NILSEN *comes to check on him.*

ARLO: [*voicemail*] Hey, Gen, just checking in. I haven't heard back—

GEN *stops the voicemail.*

JAZZ SINGERS *start to scat to Paul Kelly's 'Dumb Things'. The McMahons HATE it.*

GEN, ROSIE *and* DAD *line dance. It is slick! They high-five!*

DR NILSEN *and* TONY *shake hands and* DAD *sits down to take a moment alone.*

SCENE TEN

TONY, CAROLYN, DAD *and* ROSIE *sit on deckchairs. An opened box and torn wrapping paper are strewn across* CAROLYN*'s lap.*

CAROLYN: I will be booking this facial next week. What a thoughtful gift, Hamish.

DAD: I remember how much you liked that place.

CAROLYN: Good memory. Where's Gen?

ROSIE: She had a call.

DAD: She's gone?

ROSIE: Yeah.

DAD: Right, okay. I best be off too then. Happy birthday. Bye, possum.

DAD *kisses the girls on the cheek and farewells* TONY.

TONY: See ya, mate.

DAD: Yeah bye. See you soon.

ROSIE *hugs* CAROLYN.

TONY: Right, I'll clean up shall I?

ROSIE: Tu l'as bien dressé. (You trained him well.)

CAROLYN: [*laughing*] Tellement d'années. (So many years.)

ROSIE *laughs and starts rummaging through her bag.*

TONY: This feels like it's about me.

CAROLYN: Merci. Thank you for cleaning.

ROSIE: I have another gift for you. You too, Tony.

ROSIE *presents a painting from Fenix. It's a mixture of bright smears of paint across the page with 'Nan and Pop' written underneath. Pop wears a pilot uniform.* TONY *and* CAROLYN *beam.*

CAROLYN: Oh, I love it!

> *Beat.*

But did we decide on Nan? I was thinking Grand-maman.

TONY: Darling, you're not French.

CAROLYN: Nan feels like an old person. I had a nan, but I'm not a nan. I'm Grand-maman.

ROSIE: C'est parfait.

TONY: I'm very happy with Pop, because I'm not a wanker. I'll hang this on the fridge. Thanks, Ro.

> TONY *gives* ROSIE *a kiss on the cheek and leaves.*

CAROLYN: It's been so lovely having you down here so much.

ROSIE: Yeah, it's been so nice.

CAROLYN: Are you missing Fenix?

ROSIE: Yeah, I am. It's just been bad timing I guess … there's been so much to come back for at the moment.

CAROLYN: Mmmmm … there is. It's good you're here.

ROSIE: I do have mum guilt though.

CAROLYN: Ha! You'll be feeling that for the rest of your life. That is now part of your DNA. Always something you could have done differently or better.

ROSIE: Oh great, fun.

CAROLYN: Just wait till he talks back to you. Then you'll learn about all your failings that you didn't even know about.

ROSIE: I think that's on you for making us headstrong. You actually did this to yourself.

CAROLYN: And I wouldn't have it any other way.

> ROSIE *tries to bring herself to say something.* CAROLYN *puts her out of her misery.*

Shall we FaceTime my little Fenix?

ROSIE: Absolutely! You can try and teach him how to say Grand-maman.

SCENE ELEVEN

DAD *returns home.* GEN *is already inside and glances between her phone and her laptop.* DAD *watches for a moment, then gets out his own phone and types out a text. A loud DING from* GEN'*s phone. She reads the new message and looks up to find* DAD.

GEN: Yes, I can make you a cup of tea.

> *They move over to the tea things. Before* DAD *can get to it,* GEN *picks up the teapot.*

DAD: Gen, it's nine p.m. Get off your phone.

GEN: This is still early.

DAD: Genevieve—

GEN: Oooooh full name, getting serious.

DAD: It's not funny. [*Composing himself*] Can you—why don't—[*Trying to find the right words*]. Phone goes down at six p.m.

GEN: That's not really how it works.

DAD: When you're here, phone goes down at six p.m.

GEN: And lights out by six-thirty.

DAD: I'm being serious—

GEN: Why does the teapot have a blue dot on it?

DAD: Rosie's blue, you're yellow. You always have your head buried in that thing—

GEN: Why?

DAD: Just keeping track of things. Rosie's always loved the teapot. Don't worry, I've put a yellow dot on the painting above the fire.

GEN: Oh fuck no—this is really morbid!

DAD: It's not morbid, I'm just being practical. For when I—

GEN: One day.

DAD: For when I one day.

> GEN *notices something and storms to the other side of the room.*

GEN: Who's red?

DAD: Fenix.

GEN: Fenix gets the rocking horse? Grandad made it!

DAD: Exactly. It's special.

GEN: EXACTLY, IT'S SPECIAL!

DAD: It should be used, possum. What are you going to do with it?

GEN: But Fenix—he's—he's—

DAD: He's my grandson, yes. Side note, when you find a box with an orange dot: do not look inside that box. Destroy it immediately.

GEN: What's—

DAD: Immediately. Now I want to talk about my will.

GEN: Okay.

DAD: Sit down.

GEN: It's fine, Dad, I do contracts all the time.

DAD: You're not the executor.

GEN: Rosie won't want to—

DAD: Carolyn's the executor. I always thought she would be, back when we got married. So, I guess some things do work out.

GEN: Dad, I can do this—

DAD: No, darl. This is what I want. She knows my wishes, knows where the documents are. Knows the ins and outs of my business. You girls don't need to worry about all that adult stuff.

> DAD *stands, retrieves a strip of stickers from his pocket, and puts a yellow one on* GEN*'s forehead. He leaves.* GEN *puts the sticker on a wine bottle and pours herself a glass.*

SCENE TWELVE

GEN: [*to audience*] Somehow, it's September. It's been a lot of airport lounges and motorway coffee and yellow dots and finding so much Nemo. Tonight's plan: help Rosie be the queen of her high-school year.

> *Bass-heavy music plays from inside the local pub.* GEN *is buzzing. She's dressed* ROSIE *in a very revealing dress. As* ROSIE *fiddles with the length, it makes her cleavage more noticeable, so she pulls it up. This makes the dress shorter. She gives up.*

ROSIE: I don't think your dress works on me.

GEN: What are you talking about? It's great! PS thanks for inviting me.

ROSIE: Pretty sure you invited yourself.

GEN: Now, game plan: you are dating a shipping heir.

ROSIE: What?

GEN: He flies you around the world to teach French to the children of UN diplomats.

ROSIE: That feels unnecessary.

GEN: You're immune to the stuffiness of your forgotten peers, you're a childless free spirit.

ROSIE: I'm not childless.

GEN: Repeat after me— I. Am. Exciting.

ROSIE: I am exciting.

GEN: I am not going to be nervous.

ROSIE: I'm not nervous.

> GEN *leads* ROSIE *to the bar.*

GEN: I can't wait to see who has a receding hairline!

> *The music morphs into one of Dad's records.* CAROLYN, TONY *and* DAD *are deep in a convivial conversation at Hamish's house. They are smoking a joint. A few more coloured dots have appeared on various items.*

CAROLYN: Ooh, I know, never have I ever urinated in public.

> TONY *and* DAD *take a sip.*

Disgusting, both of you. I'm still winning. Hmmm. Never have I ever … flown a plane.

TONY: [*taking a sip*] That's not fair!

CAROLYN: Life's not fair, sweetheart. Never have I ever … had sex with Carolyn.

> TONY *and* DAD *look at each other, clink their glasses and drink.*

DAD: Okay, smartie—never have I ever trespassed.

> *Pause.* CAROLYN *sighs and takes a sip.* TONY *is aghast.*

TONY: What??

CAROLYN: Would we call it trespassing?

DAD: Officer Bailey called it trespassing.

TONY: Carolyn-with-a-Y, did you get arrested?!

> CAROLYN *and* DAD *are in a fit of giggles.*

CAROLYN: He wasn't a real police officer! He was campus security! It was at uni … we'd been out—

DAD: —Just, oh, so drunk. All of us—

CAROLYN: —Exam time—

DAD: —Carolyn realised she'd got the final essay question wrong, so she decided it would be a good idea to break into her lecturer's office after hours and change her answer, but she got caught by security!

CAROLYN: You could have come and saved me!

DAD: We were all still yahooing, we didn't even notice she'd gone. We weren't together at this point, I might add.

TONY: I'm married to a criminal.

DAD: I have not thought about that in years.

They laugh and enjoy the moment as TONY *stands up.*

TONY: Another beer, Hamish?

DAD: Ahhh can you grab a bag of chips from the pantry?

TONY: Coming up.

TONY *leaves.*

Back at the reunion inside the local pub. CAROLYN *and* TONY *each play different members of* ROSIE*'s high-school year.*

ROSIE: [*to audience*] This is so weird. I'm immediately eighteen again.

GEN: Oh my god, it's Marie Nicole Maddison. Never trust a person with two first names, and she has three! What should we do with her?

ROSIE: Okay, Gen—

GEN: Burn her at the stake!!

ROSIE: Hi Marie!

GEN: Nicole Maddison!

ROSIE: Trevor Goodwinkle! He has not changed one bit.

GEN: I will procure alcohol.

ROSIE *waves as* TREVOR *approaches.* GEN *leaves.*

TREVOR: Rosie McMahon!! How the bloody hell are you?

ROSIE: It's so nice to see you. What do you do with yourself now?

TREVOR *laughs. Surely she knows.*

TREVOR: You haven't seen my face on the buses? Trevor Goodwinkle, Ray White Real Estate. Let me know if your dad ever wants to sell his house. Park Crescent is a real hotspot at the moment.

TREVOR *hands over his card as* GEN *returns with alcohol.*

CAROLYN: Never have I ever … had cancer.

CAROLYN *pushes the bottle towards* DAD.

DAD: Better not let the girls hear you say that.

CAROLYN: Oh yes, of course. Should you be drinking with your deathly alcohol poisoning?

DAD: I've been thinking, it may be—

CAROLYN: Yes.

DAD: I think it's time we tell them—

CAROLYN: Yes. Yes, Hamish. I am unmoved on my stance. You should have told them a long time ago.

DAD: I know, I know. It just wasn't the right time before Christmas and then so many things changed, and it was all … just not the right time.

CAROLYN: Well it's never the right time for a lot of things. For illness, for children. For secondments.

DAD: They were having fun, I liked seeing them have fun.

CAROLYN: I understand that, I do. I want you to have this. But I can't keep being the bad guy, I can take a lot … but not about this. This isn't mine.

DAD: You're not the bad guy.

CAROLYN: Ha! Can you tell Gen that? She doesn't need tangible reasons to be angry with me, they seem to just materialise on their own and Rosie gets dragged along.

DAD: That's just what children do, Carolyn.

CAROLYN: Daughters are harder on their mothers.

DAD: They'll come round, deep down they know you're not the bad person.

CAROLYN: They don't know that, Hamish. I need this to come from you. It's the only way they'll come back to me.

DAD: They will come back to you. I mean—they're going to have to, aren't they? When I'm gone?

A long pause—did he really just say that? Eventually, she stands. She needs a break from this and wanders down to join the reunion scene.

GEN: Reckon Gus is coming tonight? He's on Tinder, so he's single …
ROSIE: Yeah, and I'm not.

> MADAME BURGESS, *high-school French teacher, approaches.*
> GEN *can't place her.*

MME BURGESS: The McMahon girls!
ROSIE: Madame Burgess!
MME BURGESS: Rosie, I heard you became a teacher!
ROSIE: Oui, j'avais la meilleure professeure. (I had the best teacher.)

> *They laugh.* GEN *laughs too, even though she has no idea what's happening.*

MME BURGESS: That's really special. Au revoir, Rosie. [*To* GEN] Bye, Jane.

> MADAME BURGESS *smiles and walks off.* GEN *sculls her drink.*

GEN: I'm going to get another.
ROSIE: Gen, slow down a bit. Let's not repeat my Year Eleven formal.

> *The following interactions happen as a seamless montage as the chaos builds. Two girls squeal and run over to* ROSIE.

HIGH-SCHOOLER 1: I love the ring!!
HIGH-SCHOOLER 2: I don't remember you in this year?
ROSIE: It was so crazy. We found out about Fenix when he was already one.
HIGH-SCHOOLER 3: I'm a midwife.
GEN: Cooooool!! Want a shot?
HIGH-SCHOOLER 3: No thanks, I'm on call.
ROSIE: He's such a great little kid.
HIGH-SCHOOLER 2: Do you have photos?
GEN: No, I'm not married.
ROSIE: Yeah, absolutely. Do you have any kids?
GEN: Rosie needed some support so I'm her date.
ROSIE: Did you go to Carcassonne?
GEN: Oh fuck no, I'm not married.
HIGH-SCHOOLER 4: Absolutely stunning!
ROSIE: ISN'T IT!! The history of the crusades is …
HIGH-SCHOOLER 4: Chilling.
ROSIE: Exactly.

GEN: Why aren't I married? Just lucky, I guess.

ROSIE: I remember that!! He came back to school with just one eyebrow.

HIGH-SCHOOLER 5: We were all terrified of sleepovers after that.

> GEN *dances over to interrupt* ROSIE *talking to* SCOTT RILEY.

SCOTT: Yeah it's been a wild ride, but nice to be back.

GEN: Scott Riley! Did you know Rosie used to have a big crush on you?

SCOTT: Is that right?

GEN: Pretty sure you're who she'd do pillow practice kisses with.

SCOTT: Ahh, haha. I probably did the same thing. And hey, really sorry to hear about your dad.

> GEN *is stunned.*

GEN: Excuse me?

SCOTT: I do some physio work with the Huskies and they're all really rooting for him.

> CAROLYN *has to head back to reality. She leaves the reunion scene and, in her own time, heads back over to* DAD.

CAROLYN: [*matter-of-factly*] Do you need any groceries this week?

DAD: No, still got lots of frozen dinners.

CAROLYN: And nothing to pick up from the chemist?

DAD: All set for delivery tomorrow.

CAROLYN: Okay. I'll pick you up Thursday for your appointment.

DAD: That'd be great, thank you.

> TONY *enters holding two bags of chips.*

TONY: Do you want Tuscan sea salt or paprika and chilli?

ROSIE: [*waving after* SCOTT] Thanks. Thanks Scott.

GEN: What an arsehole. Two-bloody-first-names Scott Riley. Also, excuse me but what nosey fucking nurse has been blabbing shit all over town.

> *Gen's phone dings.*

Whoops, I have a presentation tomorrow.

> *Beat. She laughs. She continues talking to no-one and everyone.*

Don't worry, I do my best work hungover, baby!

> *She makes guns out of her hands, shoots them and puts them in fake holsters before dancing away.*

Bianca, still working at Domino's?

ROSIE *is left by herself just watching* GEN. *She shakes her head.*

ROSIE: Jesus.

Beat.

Gus just walked in. He's walking over. I am frozen in space, but I can feel I am smiling. And it's like—there she is. *There's* Rosie. He says, 'Wow, Rosie. Hi. It's so good to see you. You look—' So do you.

We stare at each other. I think we're both thinking the same thing. Remembering the last time we saw each other. The spare room at a house party, years ago. We stayed up talking into the night. We moved closer and closer. Our faces so close, playing chicken as to who would move first.

He smiles and says 'I heard you're into Motocross now?' 'Oh what, no. That was a lie.' 'Oh! Honestly, if you were I'd believe it. You've always been so adventurous.' 'Me? Adventurous?' 'Yeah. You broke up with me so you could study five hundred kilometres away in a city where you knew no-one. That's adventurous.'

And suddenly I am thinking about his lips. I know how they feel. I remember how he grabbed me. What if tonight, I'm not me? What if I am the girl who moved away, who maybe could potentially do Motocross one day? Tonight, I'm not eighteen-year-old Rosie. I'm not any part of Rosie. Tonight, I can be the person whose dad doesn't have cancer. Gus leans forward and kisses me. And I … don't stop it.

SCENE THIRTEEN

GEN *and* ROSIE *walk home.* GEN *is very drunk, verging on manic.*

GEN: [*to audience*] We wobble back home high on life and kisses with high-school crushes.

ROSIE: I just … I just did it!! And it was a good kiss! It felt good! I don't know what happened, he looked at me in that same silly, cheeky way as that night. But that's bad! Oh God it's so bad.

ROSIE / GEN: I feel so alive. / Bye bye, Markus!

ROSIE: What do you mean?

GEN: Let's call him now?

ROSIE: Gen, I'm not going to tell him. This was a blip, a moment of—
ahhhhh.

GEN: You're not happy.

ROSIE: I am happy. I love Markus.

GEN: No you don't. I am so proud of you. My little sister deserves
a spark. Markus is not a spark. Markus is a damp campfire.

ROSIE: I think it's time for bed, Gen.

GEN: [*shouting at the sky*] We should alllllllll leave our Markuses, live
in a commune and send wishes to the stars.

ROSIE: Okay.

GEN: Oh oh oh, Rosie, let's make a blanket fort!

ROSIE: No.

GEN: Oh come on. Rosie … Rosie, come on let's get all the pillows and
the second mattress and make it THE BEST FORT EVER!! Do you
want to? Why don't you want to?

ROSIE: Yep, okay. I'll meet you in your room.

GEN *stumbles off stage to bed as* TONY *appears from another
room. Time slows down.*

TONY: Hi, Ro.

ROSIE: Tony? You scared me.

TONY: Yeah, sorry, I was trying to do heavy footsteps, so you'd hear
me, but that felt weirder.

ROSIE: What are you doing here?

TONY: Ahhh—

ROSIE: Where's Dad?

TONY: He's fine. He's okay. He's at the hospital.

Beat.

ROSIE: Okay.

TONY: He's fine.

ROSIE: How long have you known?

TONY: We were just with him tonight and—

ROSIE: Tony.

TONY: … Before Christmas. The whole time.

ROSIE: Of course you have. It's not good is it?

TONY: No.

Beat.

ROSIE: Right, yes … Well, I thought so. Okay right. Shit.

> ROSIE *buckles, swiftly recovers and goes into business mode.*

Okay, should we head there?

TONY: He's asleep now, Carolyn is staying with him tonight.

ROSIE: Mum's there.

TONY: Yes. She'll call if there's another update.

ROSIE: Okay.

TONY: Did you want to tell Gen?

ROSIE: Ahhhh. No. Not right now.

> *Beat.*

TONY: I've boiled the kettle.

ROSIE: Umm yeah. Thank you.

TONY: Did you have a good night? I remember my first reunion. Everyone was exactly the same. Same people wouldn't talk to me, same people gossiping about the same people. The life you make AFTER high school, that's what's important.

SCENE FOURTEEN

Hamish's house, the next morning. CAROLYN *walks in to find* TONY *and* ROSIE *at the kitchen table.*

TONY: Morning, love. How are you?

> CAROLYN *lets out a little sigh.*

Oh, love.

CAROLYN: [*to* ROSIE, *trying to shake it off*] Did you have fun last night?

> ROSIE *gives a weak little nod and watches a Berocca fizz in her water bottle.*

Where's Gen?

ROSIE: Not up yet.

CAROLYN: You haven't spoken?

> ROSIE *shakes her head.* CAROLYN *starts to mentally prepare.*

Right.

TONY: What are you going to say?

CAROLYN: I'm guessing she's going to do a lot of the talking.

TONY: What can I do? Will it be better if I'm not here or if I am part of the conversation?

CAROLYN: Oh, darling, you're a lamp at this point.

TONY: Understood.

> CAROLYN *busies herself making tea or clearing the table—anything to keep occupied. The trio is silent, but offstage there are loud clattering noises from a hungover* GEN. *She enters, phone in hand, and takes a swig from Rosie's Berocca water.*

GEN: Do you all live here now?

> *Beat.*

Where's Dad?

CAROLYN: He's at the hospital—

ROSIE: He's okay—

GEN: Okay. Let's go now—

CAROLYN: Yes. Of course, we can all go.

GEN: No, not you. Rosie and I.

> *Beat.*

Can I borrow your car?

CAROLYN: I think it'd be best if we all go.

TONY: I'm happy to drive you.

GEN: Stick to planes, Tony.

CAROLYN: Darling, I understand you're upset.

GEN: I'm not upset.

CAROLYN: You are upset.

GEN: [*to audience, HSC style again*] TENSION!

> *Annoyed that* ROSIE *hasn't joined in her HSC address to the audience like usual,* GEN *tries again.*

Rosie, oi! TENSION.

ROSIE: Gen—

GEN: Talk to me like a person, not a parent.

CAROLYN: I am your parent.

GEN: [*to audience*] DRAMA! [*To* ROSIE] Rosie, DRAMA!

> ROSIE *doesn't react. Instead:*

ROSIE: Gen. Dad's stopping treatment.

Pause. GEN *turns to the audience again HSC style, but nothing comes out. Eventually—*

GEN: What's happening here?

CAROLYN: He's stopping treatment—

GEN: I heard that.

ROSIE: Mum and Tony know, everyone knows.

TONY: I'm sorry, Gen.

CAROLYN: Let's sit down—

Just like ROSIE *did,* GEN *buckles but swiftly rallies.*

Hamish has stopped treatment, Gen. It could be … it could be a couple of months.

TONY: Things can change so quickly.

CAROLYN *waters the plants with an old glass of water.*

ROSIE: It's not fair.

TONY: I know, sweetheart.

GEN: Don't call her sweetheart, she's not your daughter.

CAROLYN: Genevieve.

GEN: So you know, you know and you know? Okay.

Beat.

Does Fenix know?

GEN *laughs.*

GEN: This is really shit.

CAROLYN: Yes, Gen—

GEN: No. You! You knew and didn't say anything.

TONY: That's not what's important right this minute.

GEN: Hmm, beg to differ, Tone.

CAROLYN: Gen, you're hanging on to the wrong thing here. Your father is—

GEN: You get to live here and see him and be here and make all of your decisions with one hundred percent of the information and what— we just fly in, fly out, take him to a festival and in our world, in our life, it's all fucking fine?

CAROLYN: That's what your dad wanted.

GEN: When have you ever cared about what Dad wanted?

CAROLYN: Well, what about what I wanted? You didn't want me involved. Cast me aside so you could play make-believe games with your father.

GEN: Oh what a surprise, suddenly it's all about you!

CAROLYN: I would love any of this to be about me! I would much rather be entering the cake competition or watching footy than doing late-night calls to check the nausea has subsided, or cooking bloody mountains of casseroles and soups! Do not tell me I have made this about me.

GEN: Now that you're divorced you care about him? I think the 'in sickness and in health' part of your vows kicked in a bit too late, Mum.

CAROLYN *clears* TONY*'s tea mug.*

CAN YOU STOP TOUCHING SHIT!!

CAROLYN *storms offstage.* GEN *smirks.*

Ah, doing what she does best. Leaving. Tony, give me your keys.

But barely a moment later CAROLYN *is back, brandishing her diary.*

CAROLYN: Would you like to see my Cancer Calendar, Gen? Monday twenty-second: remember to pick up Hamish meds. Also arnica tablets for bruising. Tuesday twenty-third: cleaner booked for eleven at Hamish's. Make sure spare key is out. Thursday twenty-fifth: ooh fun one! The wine festival! Just kidding. Lung-function test. Blood test. Monday twenty-ninth: blood test results. Doctor Nilsen, noon. Schedule ECG. Now this is just a business-hours planner, so I haven't written down 'midnight: go over to your ex-husband's house because he's too weak to get to the bathroom'. 'Google best stain-remover for vomit.' 'Note to self—ask T to pick up eggs and also H at hospital.'

TONY *looks straight ahead.*

ROSIE: I wanted to tell you.

GEN *looks at* ROSIE, *betrayed.*

GEN: We made that decision together.

ROSIE: No, we didn't.

GEN: That's not what happened!

ROSIE: You made the decision and I went along with it. Little baby sister Rosie following big sister Gen around. We needed to tell Mum!

CAROLYN: I didn't need to be told! We've known the whole time. But I wanted you to want to tell me.

GEN: Well, I wanted you to not leave your family.

CAROLYN: I did not leave. You didn't follow.

GEN: Ooh, rewriting the narrative I see?

CAROLYN: [*over* GEN] Why don't you talk to your father about rewriting the narrative? I'm not apologising any more. Take it up with him.

TONY: Carolyn did not abandon—

GEN: Stay out of it, Tony, this is a family matter.

ROSIE: GENEVIEVE.

   Beat.

You get that I'm a step-parent, right? And when you shit on Tony, you're shitting on me. And Fenix. Your nephew. And I know you hate Markus—

GEN: I'm indifferent to—

ROSIE: Do you know that Marie Nicole Maddison has met Markus? Trevor Goodwinkle wanted to see a photo of Fenix, my family. Why are you so scared of people seeing who I really am?

GEN: You deserve so much!

ROSIE: I have so much! I love what I have! And you never asked me what I wanted. You never ask me what I want! I wanted to actually talk about what's happening. Talking. Communicating. You're on the phone twenty-three hours of the day, how can you not be good at talking? Instead, we do this elaborate bloody dance to make everything happy and funny. You've RUINED *Finding Nemo* for me, now I can never watch it with Fenix! You always need to distract from the reality of what's actually happening.

GEN: I am very fucking aware of what is actually happening.

ROSIE: Then why do you need elaborate reasons to justify coming home? Does coming back for the sake of coming back not fit in with your big fancy life?

GEN: I moved away; I am sorry that is so offensive to you.

CAROLYN: Girls—

ROSIE: If Dad didn't get sick, how often would you have come home this year, honestly?

GEN: We both don't live here, Rosie. I would have come back the same amount of time as you!

ROSIE: Guess what, Gen, that was not my first time at the Lavender, Chilli and Herb Show. I come every year!

CAROLYN: You do, love.

ROSIE: And now Markus comes, and Fenix comes. And you are missing out, Gen. The garlic seasoning is perfect on barramundi.

CAROLYN: Great on potatoes, too.

ROSIE: It is!

GEN: Rosie, I don't want to dehydrate fucking coriander. My life is not here. I have built a life and career in the city. It does not make me a bad person to come back only when I have to.

ROSIE: Well hang in there, pal, Dad's gonna die soon! And once you get through the funeral you can head back to the big smoke and never return! Happy days!

GEN: Yeah and you can smoke a leg of ham with all your boring friends for the rest of your life—

TONY: That's enough!

No-one speaks. But they're all ready and loaded to fire the next round.

He's your dad. I know what it feels like to lose a dad. Nothing compares to losing a parent. I am sorry, I am sorry for what you're about to go through. But this is my family. Your mum is my family, you are both my family. And … Hamish is my friend. I am losing a really good friend, and that makes me sad. At my age those spots get harder to fill.

All four of them stay in this moment. Angry, sad and scared. TONY, ROSIE *and* CAROLYN *gather their things and begin to leave.* ROSIE *turns to* GEN.

ROSIE: Gen. If you don't come now you will always regret it.

GEN *follows.*

SCENE FIFTEEN

The hospital again. TONY *and* CAROLYN *give the girls some distance. Things are still tense between them.* GEN *is texting on her phone.*

CAROLYN: Take your time, girls.

> *They steel themselves.* ROSIE *walks into the ward but* GEN *doesn't move.* ROSIE *walks back.*

ROSIE: Gen. We'll be okay.

> *Nothing from* GEN. ROSIE *knows what to do.*

[*Said in secret silly voice*] We'll be okay.

> *A little smile. Then the girls give each other a little 'boop' on the nose.* ROSIE *leads* GEN *inside.* CAROLYN *and* TONY *walk off holding hands.*

Dad! You scared us!

DAD: I'm sorry, love.

ROSIE: How are you feeling now?

DAD: Well, I'm probably not going to be doing a lot of highland dancing in the short-term, love. Eh, Genny Gen? We'll have to give it a miss for a bit.

> GEN *smiles and nods and buries her head back in her phone. A silence. After a while,* DAD *breaks it as only a dad knows how.*

Girls, I really need to tell you something.

ROSIE: Of course, Dad. We're listening.

DAD: This is difficult to say. Um. I tried playing hide-and-seek in the hospital. But they kept finding me … in the … ICU.

> *A pause.*

The I–C–U.

> *Another pause. The girls try to compute.* GEN *finally exhales. Tension broken.*

GEN: FOR FUCK'S SAKE.

> DAD *has the giggles, he's so pleased with himself.*

ROSIE: Oh my god, DAD! That was all-time awful.

DAD: I thought it was quite good.

ROSIE: Nurse? Can we please get some more painkillers?

DAD: I'm fine.

ROSIE: They're for me!

DAD *is still cackling.* GEN *goes back to her phone.*

DAD: Okay, I'll stop. Can you both do me one favour?

ROSIE: Of course.

DAD: Go easy on your mother, okay? She is a good person. I know in your world she did this big terrible thing, but that's just not true. She's not the devil. And I'm no saint. Deal?

ROSIE: Deal.

GEN *nods her head.*

DAD: I gathered you've already figured out our little ruse. It's not looking so great. Bad luck to be honest. Thought we'd got the bugger.

I know you feel lied to. To be fair though, you've told your share of porkies. But—it was my decision not to tell you before Christmas. Maybe I got that wrong, but I'm your parent. Parents make decisions. And when things got worse, it was my decision to play along with the calendar. To be honest, I loved it. It has been bloody lovely having you here this year— to have all this time with you. Fantastic.

ROSIE *looks away on the verge of tears.*

GEN: Ah-ha!! Found her! Dad, there is this great oncologist in the city. Huge waiting list but I have pulled some strings, and she can see you on Monday.

DAD: Gen, the doctors here—

GEN: The doctors here obviously don't know what they're doing.

DAD: Oh come on, Terri—

GEN: Terri is like a hundred.

DAD: Terri and I are the same age so excuse you.

GEN: I'm going to find a medi-flight thing. I don't know if that's what they're called. I'll find a way to fly you to the city for Monday, okay?

GEN *goes to walk out.*

Do you want a seat too, Rosie?

ROSIE *goes to stand up, but* DAD *grabs her arm.*

DAD: Yep, book Rosie too, Genny Gen. Sounds good.

GEN: Okay perfect! I … need. Um charts and things.

GEN *leaves.* DAD *turns back to* ROSIE.

DAD: Just give her some time.

ROSIE: I'm mad at you.

DAD *just smiles back.*

If—if I knew earlier—Markus, Fenix and I could have moved here.

DAD: No. I never wanted that. You need to keep living your life, possum.

ROSIE: I feel stupid.

DAD: I don't. I feel lucky. Having all this time with my beautiful girls.

ROSIE: I really liked coming back.

DAD: I liked having you! The festivals! The footy! The dancing!! The cakes. We've had so much fun, haven't we?

SCENE SIXTEEN

We hear GEN *before we see her, in business mode as she finishes up a call. She pops out downstage.*

GEN: Okay, thank you. Obviously not what I wanted to hear but yes, hold the appointment. I'll figure out the flight. Okay. Thank you.

She hangs up.

Fuckers.

Gen's phone is silent for barely a second before it rings again. GEN *looks at the screen and doesn't pick up. She lets it ring out then presses on her voicemail button.*

ARLO: [*voicemail*] Um hey, legend. It's Arlo. Obviously. Just wanted to check in, I feel like something has happened, so if you want to talk about it with any of us, we're here for you. Also, maybe nothing has happened! It's just so unlike you to miss a presentation so I thought—

GEN's face falls. She scrambles to pick up the call.

GEN: Arlo, fuck! I completely forgot! Fuck! ... I just, I've had some stuff to ... you know about Dad? Fucking Deb! ... The Cancer Calendar is on the shared work drive. Of course it is. So, you all know. Well, fuck ... Yep, thank you. Is Deb there? [*To audience*] Ready to watch me beg forgiveness?

GEN's voice remains calm, but her movements become frenetic; a panic attack is approaching.

[*Back to the call*] Deb, oh my god I'm so sorry I missed the ... Yep ... No, it's just I was seeing my dad and I totally ...

She removes her blazer. It doesn't help.

... I'm so sorry, oh my god was it a total disaster? ... Oh ... *Oh*. Oh, did he? Shit, did they hate him? He's so smarmy ... they loved him? Oh, great ... Great.

She unbuttons her top button to help her breathe. That doesn't help either.

Well, I'm so sorry that you didn't have the spreadsh—oh ... Yep, sure, put him on ... Hi Brad. Congrats, sounds like it was .. ah, yep ... yep ... yep ... haha, good one. Did you get Arlo to help with ... You flew solo. That's great, Brad, well done. Well done. That's so good. Do you want me to send the follow-up? You've done it?

GEN's movements are increasingly hyper and her voice follows suit now. She paces, maybe bends over, her body desperately seeking ways to take in oxygen. She moves with the panic of someone who thinks there's a spider in their clothing, fast, furious, frenetic.

Good. That's so good. Haha no, you didn't need me at all by the sounds of it. Ha. Hahahaha. Good one. Oh cool—I love that restaurant. Well deserved. Enjoy it. I've got to go anyway actually, I've got a meeting ... no, a different one. It's not in the work drive ... You don't know them ... I've got to go. I've got to go. I'VE GOT TO GO.

GEN hangs up the phone and flings it away from her with force.

She takes great heaving breaths.

Finally, finally she crumbles to the ground beneath her.

She's out of answers.

GEN *sits in the gutter.*

SCENE SEVENTEEN

ROSIE *and* CAROLYN *arrive back at Hamish's house, emotionally exhausted. There are more dots on various items.*

CAROLYN: Tea?

ROSIE: Please.

CAROLYN: How are you?

ROSIE *shrugs.*

ROSIE: I did something bad.

CAROLYN: Do you want to talk about it?

ROSIE: I kissed someone at the reunion.

CAROLYN: Gus?

ROSIE: Gus.

CAROLYN: I always liked Gus.

ROSIE: Not helping.

CAROLYN: No, I like Markus. I love Markus. But Gus was a good first love. Are you okay?

ROSIE *shrugs again.* CAROLYN *wraps an arm around her.*

ROSIE: Sorry to disappoint you.

CAROLYN: What? You haven't.

ROSIE: It's just so … complicated. I feel like I am doing everything so badly. I'm a bad sister, bad daughter, bad caregiver, bad stepmother, bad partner. I don't know how to fix it all.

CAROLYN: You can't.

ROSIE: I am so scared of failing in every single part of my life. I'm scared about Dad, I'm scared about being a mum. I'm not there. I'm not present. He has a Markus and a Shelley, does he need a Rosie?

Beat.

CAROLYN: Want to know what was on my list? I was scared I was being a crap mum by leaving, and I was scared about being a crap mum by staying and becoming more and more unhappy, and I was scared about never taking a risk or figuring out who I was meant to be.

ROSIE: Do you regret it?

CAROLYN: I feel guilt for hurting your father, but I don't regret my decision. We were married so young, everything was set out for me, I knew what roles I had to play, and I wasn't allowed to want more. Sometimes you need to make mistakes to figure out what you should be doing.

ROSIE: Why didn't you tell us this at the time?

CAROLYN: Because you were too young, you wouldn't have understood the … intricacies, and honestly, the tedium of marital problems. Everything is black and white to children. Hamish is beautiful, a great father, lovely man. He just wasn't meant to be my lovely man.

GEN *enters the room and stands in the doorway.*

Hi Genny Gen. Do you want a cup of tea?

Beat.

GEN: I showed Dad's chart to the city doctor and they … recommended … palliative options. Make him comfortable. They were really nice. Very kind … and helpful about the whole thing.

CAROLYN: It's okay.

GEN: I couldn't get a flight. The company needed an authorised doctor to sign off on it and I … couldn't … get anyone to sign it.

Beat.

I can't do anything.

CAROLYN: No.

GEN: There's nothing I can do. So … what do I do?

CAROLYN: You can come and sit down.

Beat. GEN *walks over and sits on* CAROLYN's *lap. They hold this for a moment.*

Come here, Rosie.

ROSIE *gets on* CAROLYN's *other knee and she holds them close.*

My girls. Now my knees can only hold this for another ten seconds so I want you to know, this is going to be shit. This is going to be the most awful thing that happens. Life is cruel and it is so deeply unfair … but you will get through this.

CAROLYN *'boops' both of their noses.*

Now get up.

The girls get up. CAROLYN *goes to walk away and turns back around.*

I can take you into the hospital again tomorrow. Pick you up at ten?

The girls nod.

SCENE EIGHTEEN

DAD *enters, goes to the record player and puts on a record. 'Under the Sun' by Paul Kelly starts to play.* DAD *listens along, appreciating the music. He turns to the audience.*

DAD: That, just now, 'Under the Sun'—that was the song they should've played at the funeral. Ah. S'pose I gave it away there, but I am dead. You were warned at the top to be fair.

He sings the last two lines of the second verse of the song.

I fell in love with Carolyn to 'Under the Sun'. It would have been perfect!! But unfortunately James and Becky Harden are an acoustic folk act on weekends and they did a painfully earnest cover of 'How to Make Gravy', which would have killed me had I not already died.

I had the best worst year with my girls. My *three* girls. Sorry, Tony.

Beat.

I don't know that I was ever quite worthy of Carolyn, to be honest. She's always been … more than the girls realise. So much time wasted in fear and pride and 'what ifs'—it's hard not to get lost in the wonder of what could have been, so I just don't go there. She's a much better mum than I ever admitted. And I'm not quite as good a dad.

The bee is still in his bonnet.

Paul Kelly literally released an album of funeral songs. There are so many good ones! 'Meet Me in the Middle of the Air'. 'Deeper Water'. I'd have taken 'Dumb Things'!

He collects himself.

Rosie's last words to me were 'I need to get milk' and Gen said 'I'll be back in the morning.' It doesn't matter. They feel short-changed, of course. They didn't get the proper Hollywood goodbye. But that's life, isn't it?

My goodbye to them was how I lived with them and how I loved them. I can tell you I loved them every single second of every minute of every hour of every day. And that is really all you can hope for, to die with love. I think I was pretty damn lucky.

Seriously, 'How to Make Gravy'??

DAD *walks to the record player again. This time he plays 'Meet Me in the Middle of the Air'. After a while, he leaves.*

SCENE NINETEEN

CAROLYN *enters and stands by the record player and listens for a moment.*

TONY, GEN *and* ROSIE *enter Hamish's house carrying an array of cards, flowers and tupperware containers. They look weary.* CAROLYN *turns down the music.*

TONY: There you are, sweetheart. I'll pop the—
CAROLYN: If you say 'kettle on', there'll be another funeral soon.
TONY: ... Cork. I'll pop the cork.
CAROLYN: Good boy.

TONY *exits.*

ROSIE: Well.
GEN: Yeah.
ROSIE: That was A Day.
GEN: So many sad people.
CAROLYN: ... It was a funeral.
GEN: Yeah but I thought I would be the saddest. But fucking Kylie was more emotional.
CAROLYN: Bloody Kylie.
GEN: I got stuck consoling her at the wake, I made an excuse to leave and just didn't go back. She could be still sitting there.
CAROLYN: Good for you, Gen.
ROSIE: So much meaningful eye contact.
GEN: Right!!

ROSIE *grips* GEN.

ROSIE: 'And if you need ANYTHING, anything at all you just call me.' I don't know who you are, why would I call you?

CAROLYN: People don't know what to say, sweetheart.

GEN: Sure. Maybe there should be a book called *How to Talk to Sad People*. I'll write it. It's just one page that says: 'Talk to them normally, the end, thanks for buying the Gen McMahon story.'

TONY *enters with sparkling flutes.*

ALL: To Hamish. / To Dad.

CAROLYN: [*holding back tears*] Well, this is nice, all together. You did very well. Fenix behaved beautifully too.

TONY: You all did really well. Hamish would have loved it. Especially the showing from the Huskies!

The lack of howl is felt by everyone and it hurts. ROSIE *lets out a small howl.*

ROSIE: What did we do on the night of Pop's funeral?

CAROLYN: I stayed and cleaned up after the wake and went to bed.

Thinking about her own dad's funeral is too much. CAROLYN *wells up.*

ROSIE: Mum, I didn't mean—

CAROLYN: No, darling, it's fine. I miss your dad. I miss my dad.

A hand-squeeze from ROSIE. *Beat.*

TONY: After my dad's funeral I got blazed with my brothers.

GEN: That sounds good. Should we do that?

TONY *smirks.*

TONY: We have a small supply.

ROSIE: Really?!

TONY: It's Hamish's medical marijuana, honest, officer!

They all start laughing.

ROSIE: Great. Let's get high with Dad's cancer drugs, why not?!

TONY: I'll get it.

TONY *exits. The girls are all together. After a while—*

CAROLYN: [*in a serious tone*] Rosie, I have a wedding present for you.

ROSIE: Oh, really, Mum? That's nice.

CAROLYN: Yeah. I've booked James and Becky Harden for the reception.

Instant laughter.

GEN: Oh, fuck, if Dad wasn't already dead it would have killed him!

ROSIE adopts her best Becky Harden imitation and sings the penultimate line of the second verse of 'How to Make Gravy'.

GEN sings the following line.

Then they sing the following line together.

It's too much, they're all cackling. CAROLYN *joins in with the next two lines.*

They're all cackling like witches.

Mum, I'm surprised you know the words.

CAROLYN: First present I ever gave your father was my copy of *Under the Sun*. PK is a lyrical genius.

ROSIE: WHAT? Why don't you ever mention that? Or play his music?

CAROLYN: [*laughing*] Because I like more than one artist, girls! Right, the real tragedy of today is that my glass is dry. I'm getting another bottle.

And she's off. Beat.

ROSIE: You okay?

GEN: No.

ROSIE: Yeah, neither.

Beat.

Should we?

GEN: Yes.

GEN heads to the record player, 'Under the Sun' starts to play.

They both run out and return moments later with their childhood mattresses and start to make a fort.

The lights fade as the volume rises. The girls sing, laugh, dance and chatter.

THE END

H⊚tHouse
THEATRE

HotHouse Theatre presents a world premiere production.

The Plan (and Other Plans)
By Bridie Connell and Grace Rouvray

CAST

GEN	Grace Rouvray
ROSIE	Bridie Connell
DAD (HAMISH)	PJ Williams
MUM (CAROLYN)	Kerryn Beatty
TONY	Damian Callinan
ARLO / MARKUS (V.O.)	Nick Steain

CREATIVE

Director	Karla Conway
Production Designer	Sophie Woodward
Composer & Sound Designer	Andrée Cozens
Lighting Designer	Jasper Wood
Dramaturgy	Karla Conway
Stage Manager	Maisy Butchart
Producer	Beck Palmer

PRODUCTION

Production Manager	Beck Palmer
Lighting Consultant	Benjamin Brockman
Set Construction	Matthew Hunter Carpentry, Ken Hunter
Technical Support	Adam Boon – Professional Audio Services John Carberry, Grant Davies, Adam Elliot, Mason Wise
Photography	Michelle Higgs, Karla Conway
Documentation	Helen Newman – Nomad Films

SPECIAL THANKS

A special thanks goes to Jamie Oxenbould, Rachel McNamara, Nick Steain, Ainslie Clouston, Liam Seymour, Michael Wood, Adam Dunn, Mansoor Noor, Adam Franklin, Danny Long, Philip Jameson, Rose Maher, Liam Connell, Hattie Archibald, Julian Larnach, Clancy Hauser and Janey Paton at Belles & Whistles.

FROM THE ARTISTIC DIRECTOR

THE PLAN (AND OTHER PLANS) is a play about impermanence. That no matter how much we try to maintain control over our lives and the conditions around us, or how much we strive to craft the life we envisage for ourselves, the impermanence of things dictates that all things in life must be in constant motion. There is no arrival.

The universe throws obstacles in our path, often to force us to rise to the occasion, learn new things, build our resilience, and strengthen our capacity to grow more fully into ourselves. Sometimes to do this, we must go back and visit the past to confront challenges, reframe our thinking, find healing. Sometimes we are forced to examine inward, digging deep to find our own voice and know what we need next. The beauty of life is our capacity to experience the whole gamut of human emotions. It is a dance in constant motion. The goal at the end of life is to say no matter what happened, how or when it happened, you managed to experience it all.

In *The Plan (and Other Plans)*, all five characters go through it all, but universally they all come face to face with grief in a multitude of ways. Grief at the loss of their loved one, but also grief at the loss of time wasted in conflict, at the loss of identity, of health, of promises unkept, grief of not being accepted, and ultimately, grieving that the plan they all set out for their lives did not go exactly to plan. All the characters go through this on some level. Them and us. It is the impermanence of things that dictate this must be so.

The hilarity of this work, the joy and the humour come from witnessing the desperate striving of all the characters to fight off change, whether actively or passively, to maintain control of their lives and everyone in it. They pivot every which way you can imagine to stay ahead of the game and maintain control among the chaos.

The emotion comes from seeing them forced, to face the delusion that change is a choice. Change for all of us is an inevitability. The privilege of experiencing grief for the characters, is the knowing that they have truly experienced love.

It has been the greatest privilege to be on this journey with Grace and Bridie.

Time to head home. And hug your loved ones.

KARLA CONWAY
Artistic Director & CEO | HotHouse Theatre

A NOTE FROM THE WRITERS

Going Home is such a funny thing. No matter how old you are, there is something about hometowns and childhood bedrooms that instantly makes you start behaving like the 16-year-old who once slept there. It's a minefield. "You've changed!" Or worse: "You haven't changed a bit!" ...

The first official meeting for this work was held in 2019, drinking rosé on a balcony and brainstorming a pair of characters who would become Gen and Rosie - adult sisters thrust unexpectedly into the chaos of returning home. We spoke about what we wanted this play to be, and about our favourite elements of theatre: a cracking pace, witty dialogue, montages, music, and a heavy dose of silliness.

That balcony meeting would be our only in person meeting for the next year and a half. A global pandemic plus many other things threw the play (and our lives) into a turbulent washing machine, so the first drafts of *The Plan (and Other Plans)* were written over zoom, at times from our very own childhood homes. Which was not the plan.

Turbulent washing machines can mean you end up with different results than you expected. We expected to write the silly music montage play about regression and inheriting your parents' music taste, but the plan changed ... again. Turns out, we have written a play about seeing your parents as actual fallible humans, and the chaotic nature of grief. Not Hollywood's 'single tear rolling down your cheek looking wistfully out a window' version of grief, but the complex, unpredictable, weird, FUNNY grief that we both know well.

This work would not be here without the generous and unwavering support of the entire team at HotHouse Theatre and the Celsius Program. Thank you for the time, space, and biscuits. A huge thank you to our dramaturg and director Karla Conway who has pushed us to stretch ourselves (and our characters) ... even when we didn't want to. Thank you for your faith in us and in this piece.

GRACE: Dearest Bridie Connell, this writing partnership and our intertwined brains have produced something truly special. Thank you for exploring our dark and twisty thoughts, solving all writing problems walking laps of Sydney Park.

BRIDIE: Mate, we did it! Our play is HERE ON STAGE! Thank you for your big creative spirit and even bigger heart. Working with you has been a hilarious, enriching experience.

Lastly, a huge thank you to rosé, without which this play would not exist.

GRACE ROUVRAY & BRIDIE CONNELL
February, 2024.

BRIDIE CONNELL
Writer & Performer

Bridie Connell is a multi award-winning writer and performer. She has written and performed three one-act plays which have been performed across Australia and New Zealand.

She won the award for Best Screenplay and Best Series at Sydney Webfest for her work on the proof-of-concept webseries *Gut Feeling*, and was nominated for a host of other awards at various festivals. The series has since been picked up by ABC Iview.

Bridie was a writer and actor on *Tonightly with Tom Ballard*, and a song she co-wrote for the show won the 2018 ARIA for Best Comedy Release.

Bridie's first play was the winning entry in a high school writing competition. It toured around her native New Zealand to 25,000 high schoolers, and was just about the most melodramatic thing she's ever written (as you can probably tell from the title: *Fallen Tears*). Thankfully, she's improved since then.

Bridie is also an in-demand performer: recent acting credits include *We Interrupt this Broadcast*, *The Moth Effect*, *Ellie and Abbie* (and *Ellie's Dead Aunt*), *Pieces of Her*, *Darryl: from Beach to Snow*, *Tonightly with Tom Ballard*, *True Story with Hamish and Andy*, *Whose Line Is It Anyway? Australia* and *The Wild Adventures of Blinky Bill*. Bridie is a former national improv champion and a regular fixture in the comedy rooms of Sydney with her unique blend of character, music and improv comedy.

GRACE ROUVRAY
Writer & Performer

Grace Rouvray hails from the regional town Albury Wodonga. Since moving to Sydney in 2012, Grace has worked across writing, acting, comedy and podcasting. In 2016, Grace started a blog chronicling her thoughts and feelings on dating. Following a viral response to her blog, she turned the stories into the scripted series *600 Bottles of Wine*. The series premiered on BBC Three in 2018 and has since been acquired by Network Ten, Virgin Inflight Entertainment, TVNZ On Demand, YLE Finland, CBC Canada, ABC iview and Netflix AU/NZ.

The Guardian UK listed Grace's writing with the likes of Hannah Gadsby, Felicity Ward, Claudio O'Doherty, The Letdown, calling her "A unique and refreshing voice, great things are expected of Grace."

Grace wrote and performed the *Hour Of Power* stand up series with Katie Lees to a sold out audience at Sydney Fringe Comedy, following its success the two comedians took the show to a stand alone season at Flight Path Theatre and Adelaide Fringe online.

Her acting credits include *House of Gods, Heartbreak High, The PM's Daughter, Colin From Accounts*, biopics *House of Hancock, Brock* and Bruce Beresford's film *Ladies in Black*.

Most recently Grace has been working as a host and podcaster curating events at VIVID Sydney and working across multiple podcasts at Mamamia.

DAMIAN CALLINAN
Performer

Damian Callinan is a multi award-winning comedian, actor & writer. He is best known to audiences as the lead actor, screenwriter & co-producer of *The Merger*, the feature film adaptation of his one man show of the same name. You may also recognise his dial from his work on *Skithouse, Before The Game & Backyard Ashes* & regular guest appearances on shows such as *Spicks and Specks* & the *Melbourne Comedy Festival Gala*.

A 3-time nominee for Most Outstanding Show at the Melbourne International Comedy Festival *(The Merger, Sportsman's Night, Proxy Heroes)* he has been prolific in his output of live shows racking up awards & nominations like parking fines.

Callinan has just added author to his list of credits, with the release of a junior fiction book *Weird School*, published by Penguin Random. He also recently took out the Silver Medal for Best Comedy Australian Podcast Awards for the *The Bodgy Creek Community Podcast*.

Damian's recent screen work includes a leading guest role in the final season of *Rosehaven* [ABCTV] and a guest role on *Spreadsheet* [Paramount +] alongside Catherine Parkinson. He is also about to appear in a recurring role in the new series of *The Newsreader* [ABCTV] and has a lead ensemble role in Screen Australia funded web series *The Emu War* [Hot Dad] and *Pivot* [3 Wise Sheep]. In development, Damian has a comedy drama TV series with the working title of *Finnegan's Reef* and is working on a Kennedy, Miller Mitchell project alongside *The Merger* director, Mark Grentell.

PJ WILLIAMS
Performer

PJ Williams is a Sydney-based actor with a myriad of credits from throughout his career. PJ has appeared in films such as *Children of The Revolution, Jindabyne* and Joe Cinque's *Consolation*, as well as appearances on *Home and Away, Tricky Business, All Saints, SNOBS* and *Always Greener*.

PJ's theatre credits include *Twenty Minutes with the Devil, A Dolls House Part 2, The Diary of a Madman, Twelfth Night, The Chain Bridge, Under Milk Wood* and *The Red Shoe*.

PJ has received two Canberra Critics Circle Awards for his performances as Dr Raymond Gerrard in *The Faithful Servant* and Aksentii Propishchin in *The Diary of a Madman*, as well as the MEAA Equity ACT Green Room Award for Professional Practice.

He has been a proud member of Actors Equity since 1989.

KERRYN BEATTY
Performer

Kerryn Beatty is a singer/songwriter, actor and playwright based in Albury. A graduate of Swinburne University (Performing Arts), Kerryn has developed an eclectic career across theatre and music. Alongside her performance practice, Kerryn also works as producer for Murray River Fine Music.

Kerryn has had a long association with HotHouse Theatre and its predecessor MRPG. For HotHouse Theatre: *A Midsummer Night's Dream, Burn, Body of Desire, Embers – HotHouse 25th Anniversary Reading, Unprecedented* (Creative Development), *Last Summer* (Creative Development). For Swinburne: *Art of Success*. For AlburyCity: *Hidden Cinema*.

Kerryn's first play *Heart Story* became *HER* and was commissioned by HotHouse Theatre. It was produced in 2022 as part of HotHouse's subscription season with Kerryn performing the role of Her. Kerryn also wrote a concept album as a companion piece to *HER*.

NICK STEAIN
Voice Overs

Nick Steain is an actor, writer, VO artist, MC and comedian who studied at the Canberra Academy of Dramatic Art and 16th Street Actor Studio's in Melbourne.

For HotHouse Theatre: *Those Who Fall In Love Like Anchors Dropped Upon The Ocean Floor, This Is Your City, A Land of Snow and Ice*.

Nick co-wrote and performed in *Secrets* with Sancia Robinson at the Butterfly Club in Melbourne.

Nick also creates sketch comedy for AACTA LMAO and performs stand-up in the RAW Comedy Competition.

KARLA CONWAY
Director & Dramaturg

Karla Conway is an award-winning director, dramaturg, theatre-maker and current Artistic Director & CEO of HotHouse Theatre. She studied Theatre at the University of Missouri-Columbia, USA and graduated from NIDA (Directing) in 2009. Since then, Karla has worked professionally in numerous leadership roles, as Artistic Director/CEO of Canberra Youth Theatre, Creative Producer at Warehouse Circus, and Program Manager (Discovery & Learning) at Canberra Theatre Centre before moving to Albury Wodonga.

She has also created numerous innovative works as a theatre maker, including site-specific, and interactive live and digital gaming works for the National Library of Australia (*Retrieval*), National Gallery of Australia (*35°17˝South*) ; and adapted a board game to be played live across the twin cities of Albury Wodonga (*This is Your City - The Live Game*).

Recent works include: World Premieres - *Unprecedented* (Campion Decent), *HER* (Kerryn Beatty), and *All the Shining Lights* (Brendan Hogan), which went on to win the 2023 AWGIE Award for best Theatre for Young Audiences.

Karla is a passionate advocate for the development of artists and new Australian work, and is currently in development on a screenplay adaptation and a new Australian musical.

MAISY BUTCHART
Stage Manager

Maisy is a Melbourne based stage manager and costumier, interested in creating and working within a diverse range of live performance disciplines. Maisy is in her final year of a Bachelor of Fine Arts (Production) at the Victorian College of Arts.

Some of her recent credits include Stage Manager for *Dance Nation* (dir. Emily Tomlins), Stage Manager for Polyglot's *FLOAT* at MPavilion, Dresser for *The Magic Flute* (dir. Jane Davidson), and Costume Manager for both *Gesturing Weaving Unfolding* (chor. James Batchelor) and *Urinetown the Musical* (dir. Trudy Dunn).

SOPHIE WOODWARD
Production Designer

Sophie is a Melbourne based set and costume designer. Sophie graduated with a Bachelor of Production (Design) from VCA in 2010 winning the Beleura John Tallis Design Award in her final year.

Sophie recently designed *Fast Food, Iphigenia in Splott* and *Grace* at Red Stitch Actors Theatre and was costume designer for *Come Rain or Come Shine* at MTC. Earlier design work from Sophie includes *Hungry Ghosts (MTC), Burn One, The One* and *Mr Burns, A Post Electric Play* (FortyFive Downstairs); *Those Who Fall in Love like Anchors Dropped Upon the Ocean Floor , Between the Clouds, Pyjama Girl* and *Letters from the Border* (HotHouse Theatre); *Extinction, Rules for Living, You got Older, Uncle Vanya, The Honey Bees, The Village Bike, Wet House, Love Love Love, 4,000 Miles* and *Day One, A Hotel, Evening* (Red Stitch); *Thigh Gap, A Long Day's Dying, Conspiracy, Patient 12* and *The Savages of Wirramai* (LaMama); *Love Song* (Melbourne Fringe); and *The Sapphires, Glorious, Educating Rita, Shirley Valentine, Always Patsy Cline* and *All My Love* (HIT Productions). Sophie was Design Assistant on *An Ideal Husband* and *Twelfth Night* (MTC). In 2023 Sophie designed Campion Decent's *Unprecedented* for HotHouse Theatre.

You can view Sophie's work at www.sophiewoodwarddesign.com

ANDRÉE COZENS
Composer & Sound Designer

Andrée creates music and sound design for theatre, animation and choral and vocal music.

In 2022 she was composer and sound designer for HotHouse Theatre's *All the Shining Lights*. Awarded the Phee Broadway Theatre Creative Residency in 2021, she co-created *Cafe Cantata* with Mark Penzak for the Castlemaine Festival 2021.

Other theatre works include *I am Desert* (2017) which she was invited to perform at the Hooyong Festival South Korea, *Spookmaster* (2017), *Journey to the Centre of the Earth* (2016), *Labyrinth in the Library* and *Maia Takes Flight* (2015).

Andrée lives and works on Bpangerang country, North- East Victoria.

JASPER WOOD
Lighting Designer

Jasper has always had a love for live performance work, arts and photography, working in his first tech-role for *The Last Boy on Earth* by Brendan Hogan at the age of 12.

Jasper joined HotHouse Theatre in 2023 as a Technician for a number of productions including *HER, Listening to Voices, PlayBox, Indigo Children* and *Borderville* 2023.

For the Flying Fruit Fly Circus he worked on *Spherical* and as Stage Manager for *Over the Top* at the Wanderers Festival. Jasper works as a freelance photographer and is pursuing Lighting Design as a career path.

BENJAMIN BROCKMAN
Lighting Consultant

Benjamin Brockman (They/Them) is an award-winning lighting and set designer who has worked both in Australia and internationally.

Sydney Theatre Company: *Constellations, A Fool In Love, American Signs*; Queensland Theatre company: *Family Values*; Griffin Theatre Company: *Family Values, Splinter, Replay, Diving For Pearls*; National Theatre Of Paramatta: *Things Hidden Since The Foundation Of The World* (AUS/UK), *Lady Tabouli, Girl In The Machine, The Girl/ The Woman, The Sorry Mum Project, Let Me Know When You Get Home*; Darlinghurst Theatre Company: *Overflow, Torch Song Trilogy, Broken, Detroit, Mother Fucker With A Hat, Tinder Box*; Hayes Theatre Company: *Gentlemen Prefer Blondes, Carmen Alive Or Dead, Razorhurst*; Belvoir 25a: *Horses, Jess & Joe Forever, Greater Sunrise*; Ensemble Theatre: *Tribes, The Big Dry, The Plant, Neville's Island*; Pinchgut Opera: *Farnace*; Critical Stages: *Alphabetical Sydney*; CDP: *Are we there yet?, Guess How Much I Love You, Spot Live On Stage*; Sydney Mardi Gras Festival: *Sissy Ball 2022, Sissy Ball 2020*; Campbelltown Arts Centre: *Mirage*; Apocalypse: *Cleansed, Metamorphoses, Angels In America Part 1 And 2*; bAKEHOUSE: *Coram Boy, Dresden, Visiting Hours, The Laden Table, Jatinga*; Squabbalogic: *Day of the Triffids* (development), *Good Omens The Musica* (development), *Herringbone, Grey Gardens The Musical, Man Of La Mancha*; Little Eggs Collective: *Symphonie Fantastique*; Legs On The Wall: *Cat's Cradle, The Raft, Waters Edge*; Shaun Parker & Company: *In The Zone, King*; Dance Makers Collective: *The Rivoli*; Green Door Theatre: *Omar And Dawn*; Steps And Holes: *21 Forester Street, La Voyage*; Bontom: *Chamber Pot Opera, Chamber Pot Opera UK*;

Awards: APDG Award for best lighting design for a Live Performance or Event *(Cleansed)*, Best Lighting Design for an Mainstage Production 2023 *(Constellations)*, Best Lighting Design for an Independent Production 2019 *(Metamorphoses)*, Best Lighting Design for an Independent Production 2021 *(Symphonie Fantastique)*.

BECK PALMER
Producer

For over 30 years Beck has worked in performing arts for many companies and on innumerable productions. From volunteering in the scenic workshop of Ensemble Theatre, Sydney to cutting her teeth as a Stage Manager touring around Australia and overseas with Dancenorth Townsville - bringing performances and workshops to regional, national and international audiences and communities.

As Production Manager her highlights are: Chunky Move, REM Theatre, Marguerite Pepper Productions, Sydney Theatre Company, Soft Tread Productions, Sydney Festival, Adelaide Festival, Sydney Fringe, Bordeville Circus Festival, New Zealand Arts Festival, Wexford Opera Festival (Ireland), Brighton Comedy Festival (UK), Assembly Rooms (Edinburgh).

Beck has liaised with producers, presenters, artists, audiences and organisations for all HotHouse Theatre productions, commissions and programs since 2012.

ACKNOWLEDGMENT TO COUNTRY

HotHouse Theatre recognises Aboriginal and Torres Strait Islander peoples as the First Peoples of this land.

We acknowledge the traditional custodians of the lands upon which HotHouse Theatre stands and pay our respect to the Ancestors, Elders and storytellers, who hold the memories, traditions and cultural knowledge of this place.

We recognise the historical impact of the past endures, and we embrace our responsibility to listen deeply, care for Country, and respect the resilience and wisdom of the world's oldest continuing culture, as we journey forward together.

ABOUT HOTHOUSE THEATRE

HotHouse Theatre incubates, makes and presents 100% Australian theatre, divergent in form and voice that speaks to our region and the nation. We invest in regional professional practice. We collaborate with artists locally and nationally to engage and inspire audiences. Through shared experiences, we stimulate the imagination of the region, inspiring insight into our humanity through creative interrogations, which reflect the world around us.

HotHouse Theatre has a rich and celebrated 25-year history of commissioning, nurturing, producing and presenting new, contemporary Australian theatre within a vibrant regional setting. Created from the Murray River Performance Group in 1997, HotHouse Theatre draws on 40 years of theatre making experience in regional Australia. Located in Albury Wodonga, we serve the audiences and artists of the VIC Border North East and NSW Border Regions.

A critical national incubator of distinctive Australian theatre, HotHouse's investment in artists, audiences and community engages locally and impacts nationally.

CELSIUS: INDEPENDENT THEATRE PROGRAM

CELSIUS is an initiative of HotHouse Theatre which provides a creative home, support and investment in the development of local, independent theatre practitioners through the research, creative development phases and co-production of independent theatre works that ignite and inspire regional audiences.

This production began as a CELSIUS development in 2021 and was originally titled Growing Down. Over a three year partnership, HotHouse has supported Grace and Bridie to bring the work to completion, with assistance along the way from dedicated artists who have contributed to its development. Special thanks to Jamie Oxenbould, Rachel McNamara and Nick Steain. This production is gratefully supported by the Australian Government through its Restart Investment to Sustain and Expand (RISE) Fund.

HOTHOUSE THEATRE STAFF

Artistic Director & CEO | Karla Conway
Business Manager | Madeleine Schnelle
Producer | Beck Palmer
Assoc. Producer-First Nations | Tiffany Ward
Communications | Luke Preston
Technical Trainee | Jasper Wood

BOARD

Chair | Shaun Field
Deputy Chair | John Gibbons
Secretary | Margie Gleeson
Christopher Tooher
Graham Lamond
Tanya Finnen
Kimberley Rose
Adam Crapp

ACKNOWLEDGMENTS

HotHouse Theatre gratefully acknowledges the support of our Government Funders:

Australian Government RISE Fund · CREATIVE VICTORIA · NSW GOVERNMENT · CITY OF WODONGA VIC · AlburyCity

www.ingramcontent.com/pod-product-compliance
Lightning Source LLC
Chambersburg PA
CBHW050020090426

42734CB00021B/3349